About the Author

Born in Germany, Edgar Rothermich studied music and so... prestigious Tonmeister program at the Berlin Institute of Te... University of Arts (UdK) in Berlin where he graduated in 19... worked as a composer and music producer in Berlin, and moved to Los Angeles in 1991 where he continued his work on numerous projects in the music and film industry ("The Celestine Prophecy", "Outer Limits", "Babylon 5", "What the Bleep Do We Know", "Fuel", "Big Money Rustlas").

For the past 20 years Edgar has had a successful musical partnership with electronic music pioneer and founding Tangerine Dream member Christopher Franke. Recently in addition to his collaboration with Christopher, Edgar has been working with other artists, as well as on his own projects.

In 2010 he started to release his solo records in the "Why Not …" series with different styles and genres. The current releases are "Why Not Solo Piano", "Why Not Electronica", "Why Not Electronica Again", and "Why Not 90s Electronica". This previously unreleased album was produced in 1991/1992 by Christopher Franke. All albums are available on Amazon and iTunes, including the 2012 release, the re-recording of the Blade Runner Soundtrack.

In addition to composing music, Edgar Rothermich is writing technical manuals with a unique style, focusing on rich graphics and diagrams to explain concepts and functionality of software applications under his popular GEM series (Graphically Enhanced Manuals). His bestselling titles are available as printed books on Amazon, as Multi-Touch eBooks on the iBooks Store and as pdf downloads from his website.

(some manuals are also available in Deutsch, Español, 简体中文)

www.DingDingMusic.com   GEM@DingDingMusic.com

About the Editor

Many thanks to Tressa Janik for editing and proofreading this manual.

Special Thanks

Special thanks to my beautiful wife, Li, for her love, support, and understanding during those long hours of working on the books. And not to forget my son, Winston. Waiting for him during soccer practice or Chinese class always gives me extra time to work on a few chapters.

The manual is based on Logic Pro X v10.2

Manual: Print Version 2015-1124

ISBN-13: 978-1517631475

ISBN-10: 1517631475

Copyright © 2015 Edgar Rothermich

All rights reserved

Disclaimer: While every precaution has been taken in the writing of this manual, the author has no liability to any person or entity in respect to any damage or loss alleged to be caused by the instructions in this manual. Amazon and CreateSpace are not affiliated and in no way endorse this book.

About the GEM (Graphically Enhanced Manuals)

UNDERSTAND, not just LEARN

What are Graphically Enhanced Manuals? They're a new type of manual with a visual approach that helps you UNDERSTAND a program, not just LEARN it. No need to read through 500 pages of dry text explanations. Rich graphics and diagrams help you to get that "aha" effect and make it easy to comprehend difficult concepts. The Graphically Enhanced Manuals help you master a program much faster with a much deeper understanding of concepts, features, and workflows in a very intuitive way that is easy to understand.

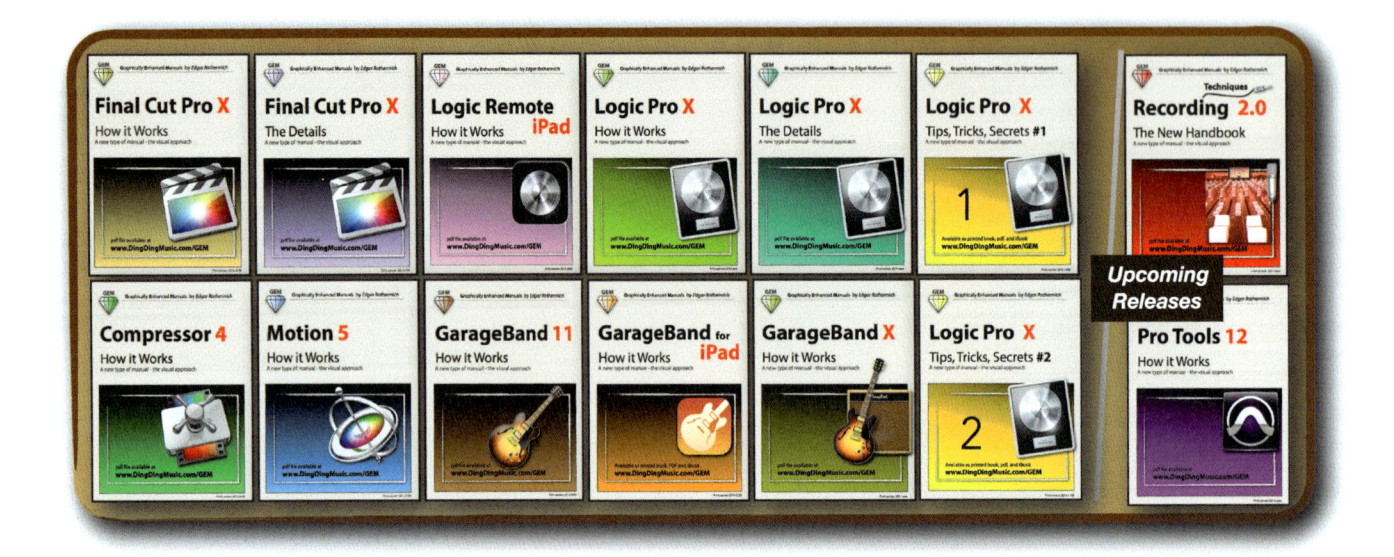

All titles are available in three different formats:

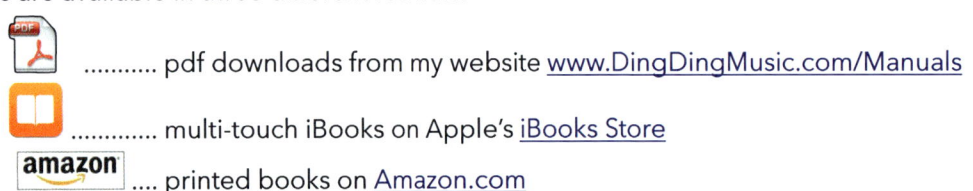

- .... pdf downloads from my website www.DingDingMusic.com/Manuals
- .... multi-touch iBooks on Apple's iBooks Store
- .... printed books on Amazon.com

(some manuals are also available in Deutsch, Español, 简体中文)

For a list of all the available titles and bundles: www.DingDingMusic.com/Manuals

To be notified about new releases and updates, subscribe to subscribe@DingDingMusic.com

About the Formatting

I use a specific color code in my books:

Green colored text indicates keyboard shortcuts or mouse actions. I use the following abbreviations: **sh** (shift key), **ctr** (control key), **opt** (option key), **cmd** (command key). A plus (+) between the keys means that you have to press all those keys at the same time.

sh+opt+K means: Hold the shift and the option key while pressing the K key.

(light green text in parenthesis indicates the name of the Key Command)

Brown colored text indicates Menu Commands with a greater sign (➤) indicating submenus.

Edit ➤ Source Media ➤ All means "Click on the Edit Menu, scroll down to Source Media, and select the submenu All.

Blue arrows indicate what happens if you click on an item or popup menu ➡

2   Logic Pro X - Tips, Tricks, Secrets #1

Table of Contents

1 - Introduction 5
About This Book 5
The GEM Advantage 6

2 - Hidden Features 9
Piano Roll 9
- Set Default Length for Note Inputs in the Piano Roll Editor 9
- Use Step Input Keyboard for Setting Note Length for MIDI In 11
- Set Default Velocity for Penciled-in Notes 12
- Create MIDI Events in the Piano Roll outside MIDI Regions 13

File 14
- Open Dialog Window Displays Additional "Media" Category in the Sidebar 14
- Special "Alias Folder" in the Media Browser 16

Tracks Window 18
- Hidden "Global Marker Track Button" 18
- Indication for the First of Multiple Selected Tracks 19
- Show/Hide "Output Track" vs. "Master Track" 20
- Capture Recording for Audio Tracks 22
- Movie File's Embedded Audio Track Plays through System Audio 23
- Color Palette Can Display Multiple Selected Colors 24
- Copy-Paste Graphics from Clipboard to the Track Icon Window 24

Mixer 25
- Three Different Input Monitoring Buttons 25
- Level Meter Reads Audio Input When Record-Enabled 26
- Input Monitoring Automatically Lowers Fader for Internal Microphone 29
- Play through Multiple Audio Devices Simultaneously 30
- "Show Only" a Specific Channel Strip Group 32
- Stereo vs. Two Mono Output Channel Strips 33
- Solo Safe on Output Channel Strip 35

Workflow 36
- Use "Go to Position Window" as Memory Locator 36
- List of All Open Windows in the Window Menu 37
- Dock and Mission Control with Logic 38

Miscellaneous 40
- How to Import/Export the Custom Configuration in the Plug-in Manager 40
- Tempo Sets Store Individual Synchronization Settings 42

3 - Special Click Actions 43
Tracks Window 43
- Close Window Panes by Double-Clicking on a Header or Divider Line 43
- Track Icons Click Functionality 44
- Create MIDI Region on an Audio Track 45
- Select/Deselect All Events on a Global Track 45
- Option+Click on a Parameter to Reset it to Default Value 46
- Choose a Flex Mode for Multiple or All Tracks 47
- Toggle Configuration Windows with Their Key Command 48
- Long Click on Primary Ruler Enables Cycle Mode 48
- Change Priority for Coloring Regions/Tracks 49
- Two Different Solo Tools 50
- Click Zone Rules for Cursor Tool in the Track Lane 51

Piano Roll 53
- Three "Priority" Tools in the Piano Roll 53
- Overwrite Min and Max Velocity Value of a Group of Notes 54
- Drag Velocity Ramp in the MIDI Draw Area 57
- Special Pencil Tool Functionality 59
- Open Score Editor or Event Float from Piano Roll 60
- Opt+Scroll to Zoom horizontally and vertically 60

Workflow
- Show a Specific Menu Command in the Key Commands Window........................61
- Double-Arrow Playhead Position Tool 62
- Three Tools - Four Tool Menus 64
- Key Equivalents for Non-Extended Keyboards..66
- Use Arrow Keys in New Tracks Dialog..67
- Use OSX Key Commands for Dialog Windows 67
- Full Screen Mode vs. "Almost" Full Screen Mode 68
- Move Windows without Making Them Active Windows......................................69

4 - Did you Know? — 70

File
- Special Proxy Icon Functionality...70
- Create Loops by Dragging Regions over the Loop Browser 71
- Delete Backup Files inside a Project...71

Tracks Window
- Logic in GarageBand Mode..72
- Batch-rename Regions Sequentially..73
- Copy Entire Track including Region and Automation 74
- Global Tracks Protect Button..75
- Tear off Floating Window Panes 76
- Remove the Group Inspector (kind of)..77

Mixer
- Change Plugins and Aux Sends on Multiple Channel Strips at Once.....................78
- Add EQ or Compressor with One Click..79
- Toggle Plugin and Sends on/off 81
- Reset Channel Strip 81
- Numerical Entry of Onscreen Controls (with Decimal Points)...............................82
- Signal Flow Inspector Channel Strip...83
- Show Aux Channel Strip of Used Bus Sends..84
- Channel Strip Solo is "Signal Flow Aware"...85

Workflow
- Key Switcher..87

5 - Be Aware! — 88

Tracks Window
- Confusing "New Track" Commands...88
- Track Name vs. Channel Strip Name..91
- "Delete Automation" Commands Are Incomplete..92

Editing
- Project Type Sets the Unit for the Delay Parameter in the Region Inspector........93
- Two Separate Values for the Delay Parameter in the Track Inspector....................94
- Cut/Insert/Repeat Section Commands have Two Variations 96
- Dynamic Functionality of the "Show Editor" Command 97

Miscellaneous
- Important Difference between Sheets and Popovers...98
- Input Focus - Consequences 100

Conclusion — 101

1 - Introduction

About This Book

This is **Vol #1** of my best-selling book series "**Logic Pro X - Tips, Tricks, Secrets**".

One thing you will often hear when people talk about Logic and exchange their experience is, "*Oh, I didn't know that Logic can do this*". The reason for this is that no matter how well you know Logic, or how many years you have been using it, there is always something new to discover.

> "Oh, I didn't know that Logic can do this"

Of course, the best way to discover all those things is to read the manual, hopefully the ones in my "Graphically Enhanced Manuals (GEM) series. But beyond that, there are so many hidden features and lesser known workflows that often get lost, or you might have never heard of them in the first place.

From Beginner to Advanced

I can guarantee you that no matter at what level your Logic experience is, you will find amazing tips and information in this book that you can put to use right away and improve your Logic experience immediately. You might fall into any of the following categories:

- ☑ You didn't know about those topics
- ☑ You heard about them, but didn't know how to use them
- ☑ You knew about them, but forgot about them

Learning Beyond the Topic

This book is not just a list of "*Logic can do xyz if you do this and click that*". Each topic has two sections:
- ▶ **Review**: This provides a short introduction for the topic, so regardless of your Logic knowledge, you will better understand what's so special about the topic. If the topic requires a deeper understanding, then I point out to one of my books where I discuss the fundamentals in more detail.
- ▶ **Attention**: This is the section where I discuss the topic. Not only will I explain the topic, but I will also provide the information in the context of the bigger picture, so the actual learning process that the reader gets from the book is far beyond the actual trick, trip, or secret.

Four Chapters

I divided the topics into four chapters:
- ▶ **Hidden Features**: These are features and functionalities that are not found in the official User Guide and are not widely known in the Logic community.
- ▶ **Special Click Actions**: These are topics related to mouse actions, clicking on areas, and using modifier keys around the ever changing Cursor Tool. Logic is full of those 'easter eggs".
- ▶ **Did You Know?** These are important and lesser known features and workflows that will improve your workflow, the way you use Logic.
- ▶ **Be Aware**: These are details of specific features that many users might not be aware of and often run into trouble or frustrations due to the lack of proper understanding.

The GEM Advantage

If you've never read any of my other books and you aren't familiar with my Graphically Enhanced Manuals (GEM) series, let me explain my approach. As I mentioned at the beginning, my motto is:

"UNDERSTAND, not just LEARN"

Other manuals (original User Guides or third-party books) often provide just a quick way to: "press here and then click there, then that will happen ... now click over there and something else will happen". This will go on for the next couple hundred pages and all you'll do is memorize lots of steps without understanding the reason for doing them in the first place. Even more problematic is that you are stuck when you try to perform a procedure and the promised outcome doesn't happen. You will have no understanding why it didn't happen and, most importantly, what to do in order to make it happen.

Don't get me wrong, I'll also explain all the necessary procedures, but beyond that, the understanding of the underlying concept so you'll know the reason why you have to click here or there. Teaching you "why" develops a much deeper understanding of the application that later enables you to react to "unexpected" situations based on your knowledge. In the end, you will master the application.

And how do I provide that understanding? The key element is the visual approach, presenting easy to understand diagrams that describe an underlying concept better than five pages of descriptions.

The Visual Approach

Here is a summary of the advantages of my Graphically Enhanced Manuals that set them apart from other books:

Better Learning

- **Graphics, Graphics, Graphics**

  Every feature and concept is explained with rich graphics and illustrations that are not found in any other book or User Guide. These are not just a few screenshots with arrows in it. I take the time to create unique diagrams to illustrate the concepts and workflows.

- **Knowledge and Understanding**

  The purpose of my manuals is to provide the reader with the knowledge and understanding of an app that is much more valuable than just listing and explaining a set of features.

- **Comprehensive**

  For any given feature, I list every available command so you can decide which one to use in your workflow. Some of the information is not even found in the app's User Guide.

- **For Beginners and Advanced Users**

  The graphical approach makes my manuals easy to understand for beginners, but still, the wealth of information and details provide plenty of material, even for the most advanced user.

Better Value

- **Three formats**

  No other manual is available in all three formats: PDF (from my website), interactive multi-touch iBooks (on Apple's iBooks Store), and printed book (on Amazon).

- **Interactive iBooks**

  No other manual is available in the enhanced iBook format. I include an extensive glossary, also with additional graphics. Every term throughout the content of the iBook is linked to the glossary term that lets you popup a little window with the explanations without leaving the page you are currently reading. Every term lists all the entries in the book where it is used and links to other related terms.

- **Up-to-date**

  No other manual stays up to date with the current version of the app. Due to the rapid update cycles of applications nowadays, most books by major publishers are already outdated by the time they are released. I constantly update my books to stay current with the latest version of an app.

- **Free Updates** (pdf, iBook only)

  No other manual provides free updates, I do. Whenever I update a book, I email a free download link of the pdf file to current customers. iBooks customers will receive an automatic update notification, and 24 hours after a new update, the printed book will be available on Amazon. They are print-on-demand books, which means, whenever you order a book on Amazon, you get the most recent version and not an outdated one that was sitting in a publisher's warehouse.

Self-published

As a self-published author, I can release my books without any restrictions imposed by a publisher. Rich, full-color graphics and interactive books are usually too expensive to produce for such a limited audience. However, I have read mountains of manuals throughout the 35 years of my professional career as a musician, composer, sound engineer, and teacher, and I am developing these Graphically Enhanced Manuals (GEM) based on that experience, the way I think a manual should be written. This is, as you can imagine, very time consuming and requires a lot of dedication.

However, not having a big publisher also means not having a big advertising budget and the connections to get my books in the available channels of libraries, book stores, and schools. Instead, as a self-published author, I rely on reviews, blogs, referrals, and word of mouth to continue this series.
If you like my "Graphically Enhanced Manuals", you can help me promote these books by referring them to others and maybe taking a minute to write a review on Amazon or the iBooks Store.
Thanks, I appreciate it:

amazon http://amzn.to/1sP8jvl   http://bit.ly/1oJ7ftQ

Disclaimer: As a non-native English speaker, I try my best to write my manuals with proper grammar and spelling. However, not having a major publisher also means that I don't have a big staff of editors and proofreaders at my disposal. So, if something slips through and it really bothers you, email me at <GrammarPolice@DingDingMusic.com> and I will fix it in the next update. Thanks!

LogicProGEM

Please check out my Logic site "**LogicProGEM**". The link "Blog" contains all the free Logic Articles that I have published on the web, and continue to publish. These are in-depth tutorials that use the same concept of rich graphics to cover specific topics related to the use of Logic.

http://LogicProGEM.com

2 - Hidden Features

Piano Roll

Set Default Length for Note Inputs in the Piano Roll Editor

➡ *Review*

When you use the Pencil Tool in the Piano Roll Editor to create new notes, then the default length of those new notes will be 1/16th notes ❶. But what if you need 8th notes or any other note length? Instead of entering those 1/16th notes and resizing them afterwards, you can change the default length to any value.

➡ *Attention*

To use a different default length in the Piano Roll Editor for newly penciled-in notes, you have to understand the following underlying rules:

💡 Set the Default Note Length Value

- ▸ Every time you launch Logic, it will use the default length of 1/16th notes ❶.
- ▸ Whenever you resize a note by *dragging* the end of the note bar in the Piano Roll Editor, you will overwrite the current default length and set the new default length to this value. In this screenshot, I resized the note to a 1/4 note ❷. Changing the note length by resizing the start of the note bar has no effect on the default note length.
- ▸ Now when you click with the Pencil Tool to create a new note, it will have that 1/4 length ❸.
- ▸ You can change the default length with this procedure at any time, but also keep in mind that resizing any notes (while editing) will automatically change that default length to that value.
- ▸ The current default value maintains when you open and close Projects until you quit Logic. Re-launching Logic will reset the default value to 1/16th again.

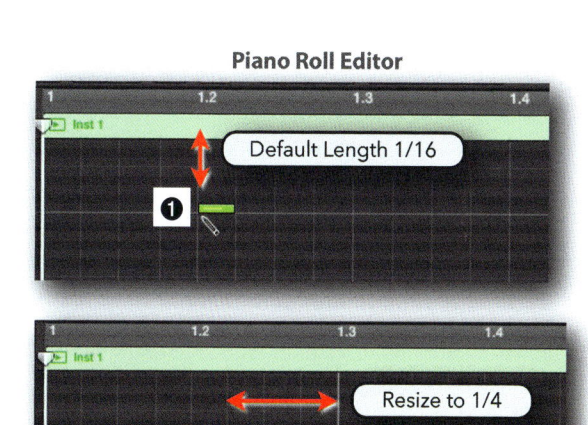

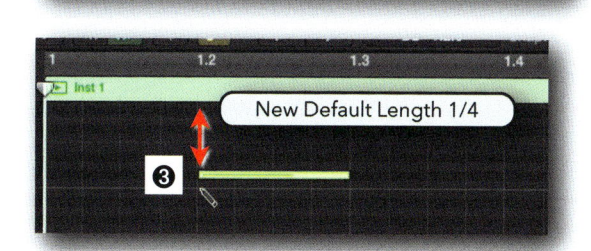

● Enter specific Note Length when creating Notes.

Instead of creating a new note with the current default value and resizing it, you can do this at the same time.

▸ Instead of just *clicking* with the Pencil Tool (which creates the new note with the current default length), you *click-hold and drag* with the Pencil Tool to the length you want. This creates the new note, but you can set its length while pressing down the mouse and dragging to the length ❹ you want in one action.

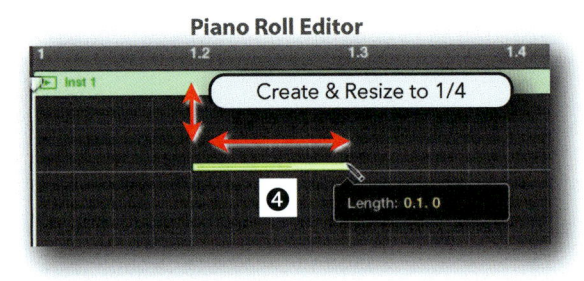

▸ This procedure also counts as a resize, which means, the length you just created becomes the new default note length.

● Other Methods to change the Default Note Length

Please keep in mind that all the following actions change the default length (and velocity) for new penciled-in notes:

▸ **Select a Note**: Each time you select a Note, its note length becomes the new default note length.

▸ **Resize a Note**: When you resize an existing Note with the Cursor Tool, the note gets selected. So technically, it meets the previous condition of just selecting a note. However, this is only true for resizing the right border. If you resize the left border of a note, then the new length of the note will not become the new default note length. You have to click on it after the resize to make it the default length (if you want).

▸ **Click+drag a new Note**: Resizing a note while creating a new note with *click+drag* counts as a "Set Default Length".

▸ **Menu Command "Define as Default Note**: *Ctr+click* on a note will open its Shortcut Menu with the command "Define as Default Note" ❺ on top. This also sets the default note length, but is kind of redundant, because by just clicking on the note, you have just set the default length already.

The Logic User Guide states that this command also sets the default Velocity and MIDI Channel of a newly created note, but I couldn't confirm MIDI Channel part.

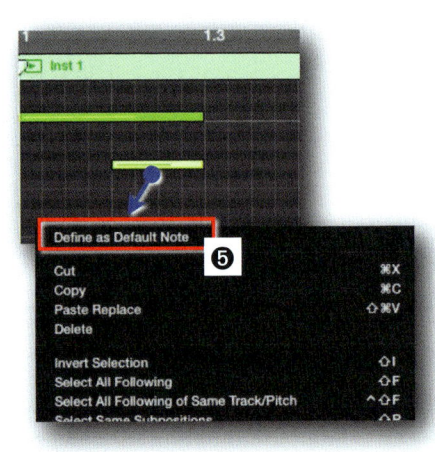

● Use the Quantize Value and the Brush Tool

There is one way to create a new note and ignore the current default length - with the Brush Tool. The length of a note entered with the Brush Tool is determined by the current Time Quantize value ❻ in the Piano Roll's Local Inspector. The good news is that you don't have to switch to the Brush Tool, holding down the shift key switches the functionality of the Pencil Tool to act as a Brush Tool.

So these are the two click actions to create a new Note with the length defined by the Time Quantize value:

   ▸ *Click* with the Brush Tool
   ▸ *Sh+click* with the Pencil Tool

Use Step Input Keyboard for Setting Note Length for MIDI In

➡ **Review**

All the MIDI Editor Windows (and even the Audio Track Editor in Flex Mode) have the MIDI In Button on their Menu Bar. It lets you enter (or change) MIDI Notes via your MIDI Keyboard in offline mode, which means, when your Project is in Stop Mode.

- **Off**: Offline MIDI In Mode is disabled.
- **MIDI In (Step Input)**: *Clicking* once on the Button toggles the "Step Input Mode". Playing a note on your Keyboard ❶ will now enter that note at the Playhead Position and moves the Playhead position to the end of the newly created note ❷, where the next note will be placed. Please note that you can also enter chords this way by simultaneously pressing multiple keys down or play them arpeggiated. Use the *tab* key to step forward without creating a note.
- **MIDI In (Overwrite)**: *Double-clicking* on the Button will switch to "Overwrite Mode". This lets you change the pitch of the selected note(s) to the pitch of the note you press on your keyboard.

➡ **Attention**

Let's look at the Step Input Method:

🎵 **Note Pitch**

The input device that is sending the Note Pitch (and Note Velocity) value for MIDI Notes can be any MIDI controller. For example, your external MIDI keyboard ❸ or any of the onscreen keyboard, like the Musical Typing ❹.

🎵 **Note Length**

When the Playhead isn't moving, then Logic doesn't know how long you are holding a specific note. Therefore, the note length information is missing and has to be determined separately. There are two ways:

- ▸ **Division Value**: The note value is determined by the Division value ❺ that is displayed in the Control Bar Display (when set to Custom Display Mode ⚙). You can change the value by *clicking* on the Division and selecting from the popup menu. There are also two unassigned Key Commands ("*Set Next Higher/Lower Division Value*") or Key Commands to set the Division to a specific value.
- ▸ **Note Symbol (Step Input Keyboard)**: This might be a faster way to visually determine the note length. If the Step Input Keyboard is open (Key Command *opt+cmd+K*), then the Division value ❺ is ignored and the note length is determined by the selected note symbol ❻ on that window.

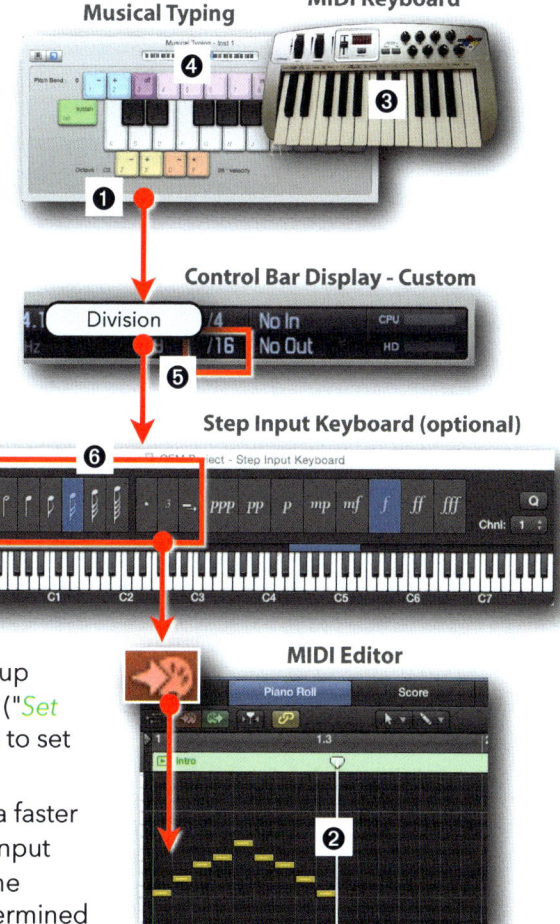

Set Default Velocity for Penciled-in Notes

➡ Review

If you record MIDI notes by playing your external MIDI Keyboard, then every Note Message contains a Velocity value (1 … 127) depending on how hard you hit the keys. However, when you manually create MIDI Notes in the MIDI Editor with the Pencil Tool ✏, then your click only determines the note value (pitch) and not the velocity. So what determines the Velocity value?

➡ Attention

The default Velocity value that is added to a manually created note in a MIDI Editor is 80. But what if you want a different value?

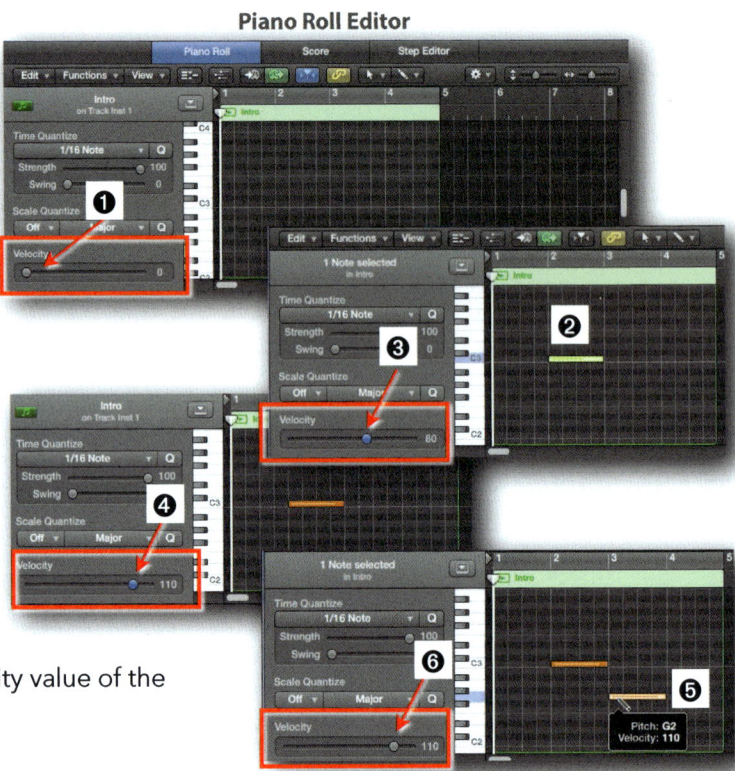

🔸 Piano Roll Editor

When you launch Logic and open the Piano Roll, then the Velocity Slider ❶ is set to 0.
- When you create your first note ❷, it will have the default Velocity value of 80, and you can see that by the position of the Velocity Slider ❸, it jumped to 80.
- Changing the Velocity value of the selected note(s) is done so by setting the Velocity Slider ❹ accordingly.
- Any newly created note ❺ gets the Velocity value of the current value of the Velocity Slider ❻.

🔸 Score Editor

A few things to keep in mind with the Score Editor:
- The Velocity Slider of the Piano Roll Editor and Score Editor are linked. Changing the position in one window is reflected in the other one.
- The procedure of setting the Velocity value is the same, it inherits the current value of the Velocity Slider ❼.
- Please note that the Local Inspector is hidden by default in the Score Editor and has to be made visible with the Local Menu command *View ➤ Show/Hide Local Inspector* ❽.

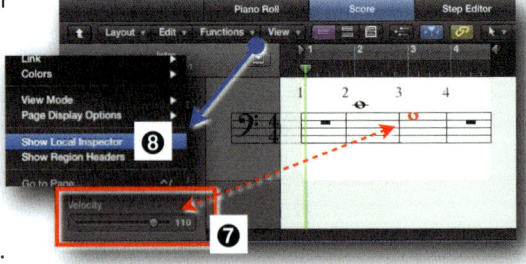

🔸 Event List

Creating MIDI Notes in the Event List is slightly different.
- When you create a new Note Event with the Plus Button, it will have the default Velocity value of 80.
- Once you change the Velocity value of any note in the Event Editor (or the Velocity Slider in other windows), that value becomes the new default Velocity value ❾, as well as for the other MIDI Editors.

Create MIDI Events in the Piano Roll outside MIDI Regions

➡ Review

You can use the Pencil Tool ✏ in the Piano Roll Editor to create MIDI Notes without being restricted to the boundaries of the visible MIDI Regions. However, there are a few rules that apply.

➡ Attention

These are the rules for creating MIDI Notes with the Pencil Tool:

- You don't need an existing MIDI Region first to create the MIDI Notes in. Whatever MIDI Track is currently selected (or was the first selected of multiple selected Tracks), will be the Track a new Region ❶ is created on with the new MIDI Note inside when you *click* on the empty Notes Area ❷ of the Piano Roll Editor.
- When there is already a MIDI Region ❸ visible in the Piano Roll Editor and you *click* up to two bars outside its right border ❹, the existing Region will be extended ❺ to include the full length of the new MIDI Note.
- If you *click* more than two bars outside the right border ❻, then a new Region ❼ will be created to contain that new MIDI Note.
- *Clicking* on any selection left of the left border, will create a new Region, unless there is another Region close to two bars on the left.
- The same rules apply if you use the Pencil Tool ✏ or the Brush Tool 🖌.

💡 One Track vs Selected Track

The Piano Roll Editor has one important setting in its Local View Menu that affects this procedure ❽:

▸ **One Track**: The Piano Roll displays all the Regions of the currently selected Track. When you create a new Note outside a Region, it will just be updated, because you are still on the same selected Track.

▸ **Selected Regions**: The Piano Roll displays all the Regions that are selected in the Workspace regardless of which Track they belong to. Here, the behavior is different:
  - When the action only extends an existing Region, then that Region is updated, but all the other selected Regions are still visible in the Piano Roll.
  - When the action creates a new Region, then that new Region will be selected and only visible, because the previously selected Regions just got deselected.

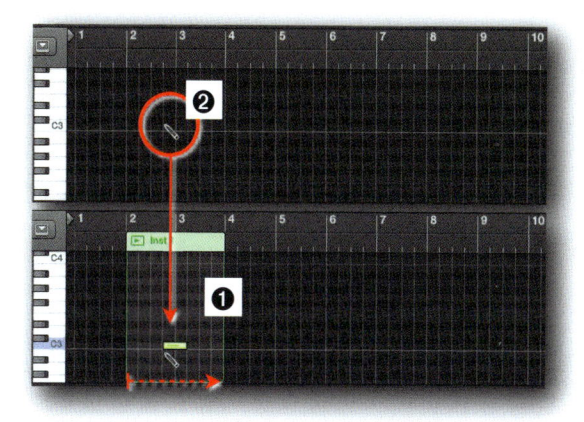

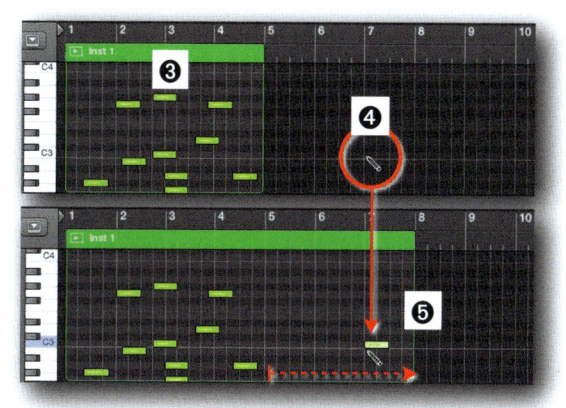

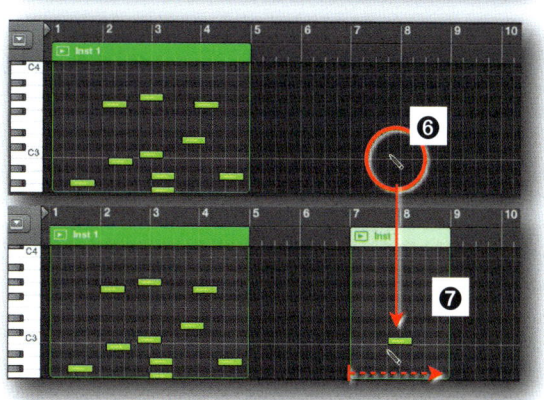

2 - Hidden Features

File

Open Dialog Window Displays Additional "Media" Category in the Sidebar

➡ Review

Here is a little recap about the Finder in OSX:

- ▶ The Sidebar ❶ in a Finder Window lists many different items that represent Devices, Volumes, Folders, or Smart Folders. You click on such an item and the Finder Window will display its content where you can drill down even further in its hierarchy.
- ▶ Those Sidebar items are grouped into four subgroups (Favorites, Shared, Devices, Tags).
- ▶ In the Finder Preferences (Finder *cmd+,*), under the Sidebar tab ❷, you can select which specific items in those subgroups will be shown or hidden.
- ▶ In the Finder Window you can move your mouse over any of those categories and a "Show" or "Hide" command ❸ appears that lets you, you guessed it, show or hide the items in that category. It works like an invisible disclosure triangle.
- ▶ You can drag the categories up and down to re-arrange the order, and also drag the items inside a category.
- ▶ The Favorites category ❹ in the Sidebar is special, because you can *drag* your own folders in (and out) to have quick access to often used folders, for example, your Logic Projects or often used audio samples and movie files. Keep in mind that the Sidebar is also displayed in any Open Dialog and Save Dialog, so any folder where you often save files to or open files from when using Logic (or any other app) is right there at your finger tips without drilling half a mile through multiple subfolder.

Finder Window

Finder Preferences

14   2 - Hidden Features

➡ *Attention*

What I just mentioned are basically considerations for your workflow when using your computer. However, the following is something special that is often overlooked in Logic:

> **Most Open Dialog Windows in Logic list an additional "Media" category in the Sidebar**

If you use the *Open Project*, the *Import Audio File*, or the *Open Movie* command, for example, then Logic will pop up the Open Dialog Window as expected. However, if you look closely, then you will see that those windows display an additional "Media" category ❶ in the Sidebar with up to three items: Music ❷, Photos ❸, and Movies ❹.

- ▸ The items in the Media category act like Smart Folders that show only files on your computer that match the selected media type.
- ▸ The Finder Window is divided into two panes on the right with additional subcategories ❺ on top and the actual files ❻ for the selected subcategory in the lower pane.
- ▸ The layout and the displayed subcategories are slightly different for the three media types and also depend on what files are available on your drive.
- ▸ The layout and functionality of the Open Dialog Window, when selecting any of the Media Categories, is similar to Logic's Media Browser ❼.

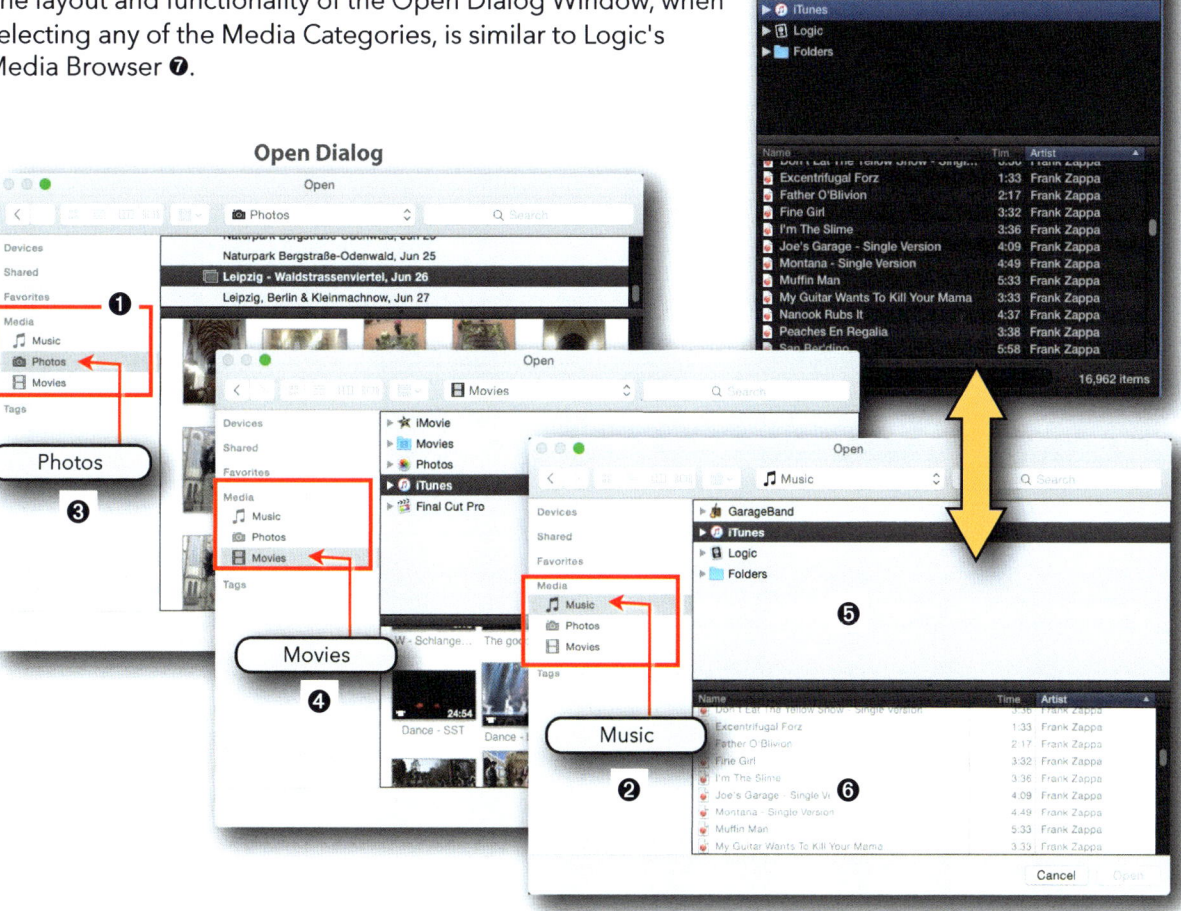

The Media Browser is living in the shadow of the other more popular features in LPX, which is unfortunate. It has a lot of powerful and useful features that are worth discovering and incorporating into your workflow. I explain this in great detail in my book "Logic Pro X - How it Works".

2 - Hidden Features   15

Special "Alias Folder" in the Media Browser

➡ **Review**

The Media Browser has some very powerful features when it comes to importing media files from your drive into your Project. Instead of using the standard Import command and navigating through your drive with the Open Dialog, trying to find a specific file, the Media Browser presents special Smart Folders. When selecting the icon for GarageBand, iTunes, or Logic in the upper window pane ❶, Logic will display all the relevant media files for that selection in the Results List below ❷, regardless where the files are located on the drive. However, there is one hidden feature that makes the Media Browser even more powerful. It is an item called "**Folders**".

➡ **Attention**

You can add your own folders to the upper section of the Media Browser. This is useful if you have audio or movie files that you often need to import into your Projects (beats, stings, logos, SFX, etc.). Now with the ability in LPX v10.2 to drag audio samples directly onto the Drum Kit Designer, you can place your organized drum samples, as folders, in the Media Browser. Here is how it works:

▶ **Drag the first folder**: You drag a folder from your Finder over the upper section of the Media Browser (i.e. SFX) ❸. A folder icon with a green Plus symbol ➕ appears under the cursor, indicating that you "add" that folder.

▶ **"Folders" item is added**: Once you release the mouse, a new item "Folders" ❹ is added to your Media Browser. When you open its disclosure triangle, it reveals the folder that you just added (SFX) ❺. When you select that Folder, all the media files in that folder will be displayed in the Results List ❻ below, where you can drag them directly into your Logic Project. At that moment you don't have to know where those files are located on your drive(s).

▶ **Drag additional Folders**: You can drag even more folders onto the Media Browser. They will all be added inside the Folders item ❼.

▶ **Display files**: You can either select a specific folder inside the "Folders" item to display its files in the Results List or select the "Folders" item itself to display all files of all folders at once ❽.

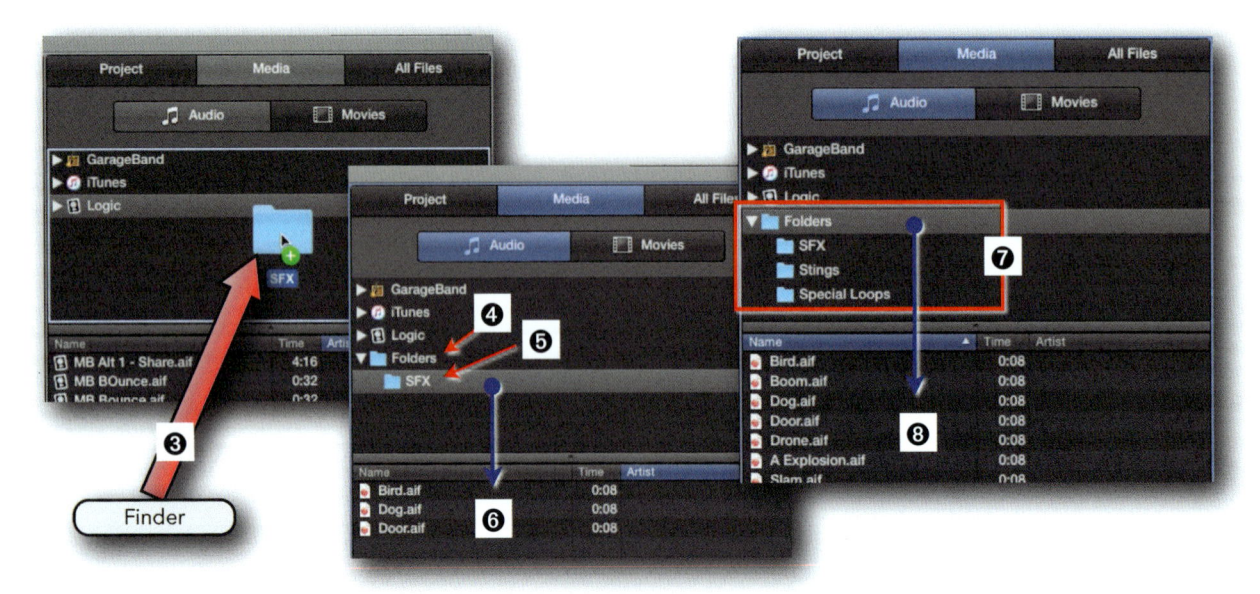

16   2 - Hidden Features

Additional Info

A few things you have to keep in mind when using this special Folders item:

- **Manage Files**: You can add, remove, and even rename the files in that folder in the Finder. Those changes are reflected in the Media Browser right away (after a second or two).

- **Empty Folder**: If one of those folders is empty, then it appears as a gray folder icon instead of a blue folder icon.

- **Rename or Move folder in the Finder**: You cannot move the folder on the Finder to a new location or rename it, it will break its connection to the Media Browser.

- **Alias Folders**: You can move, however, Alias Folders onto the Media Browser. The folder icon indicates that with the typical Alias arrow key on the folder icon.

- **Remove Folders from the Media Browser**: You can remove a folder from the Folders item by selecting it and hitting the delete key. Or you can *ctr+click* on the item and select "*Remove Folder*" from the popup menu. It also has a command to show the folder in the Finder.

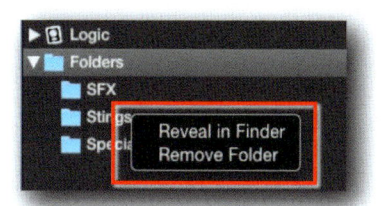

- **Importing items**: Not only can you import individual files from the Results List to your Project, you can also *drag* an entire folder onto the Project's Track Lane. A Dialog Window asks you where to place those files. You can also drag the entire Folders item to the Track Lane.

Movie Files

The whole concept of the Folders item also works under the Movies tab of the Media Browser. This Folders item is independent from the Folders item in the Audio tab, but follows the same rules.

- If you work on a movie, you can place the different Reels into one folder to have quick access to those movie files, or place the different versions of a movie in one convenient folder.

- Remember that the purpose of the Media Browser is to display only relevant files (audio files or movie files) and ignore other file types. That means, you can use one folder to have all your audio and video files for a project in, but by selecting the Audio or Movie tab, it displays only those matching files in the Media Browser.

2 - Hidden Features

Tracks Window

Hidden "Global Marker Track Button"

➡ Review

Logic Pro X versions prior to v10.1 had a Global Marker Track Button ❶ next to the Global Tracks Button ❷. Now, the Marker Track Button is gone ❸, or is it?

💀 Global Tracks

Here is a quick recap about Global Tracks:

- The Global Track Button ❷ toggles the visibility of the Global Tracks. You can also use the Key Command *G*, or use the Menu Command *Track ➤ Global Tracks ➤ Show/Hide Global Tracks*.
- There are a total of seven Global Tracks ❹ and you can configure which ones are displayed. Use the individual Show/Hide Commands or the Configure Global Tracks Popover Window (*opt+G*).

💀 Marker Track

- The Marker Track Button was just a convenient way to quickly show just one Global Track, the Marker Track ❺.

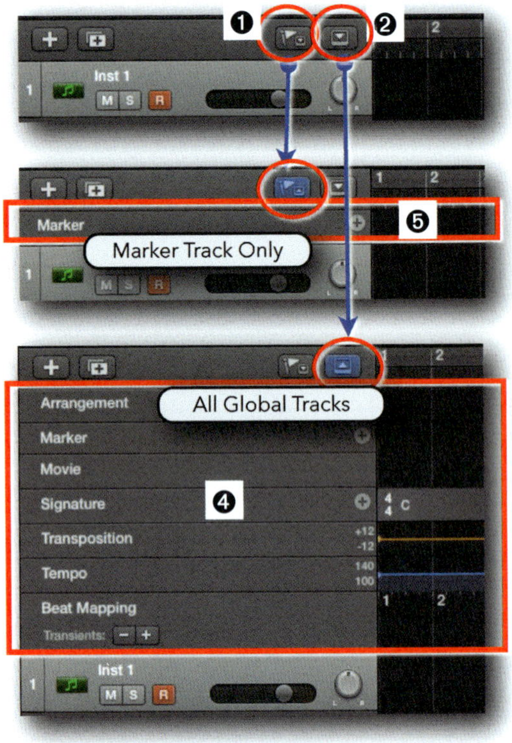

➡ Attention

Due to popular demand, LPX v10.1 again displays any Markers directly on the Ruler ❻ without the need to open the separate Global Marker Track. That might have led to the decision to remove that button. However, keep in mind that you still need to open the Global Marker Track ❼ to edit the Markers. For that reason, it would actually be nice to have that separate Marker Track Button to quickly open just the Marker Track.

💀 Show/Hide Marker Track Only

Although the button is gone, the functionality is still available as a Key Command (*Show/Hide Marker Track Only*) ' (the apostrophe key) ❽. So, whenever you want to edit the Markers, you just use that Key Command to toggle the Global Marker Track without displaying the rest of the Global Tracks at that moment.

The other command *Show/Hide Marker Track* (*sh+cmd+K*) toggles the visibility of the Marker Track ❾ when you display it with the Global Tracks Button.

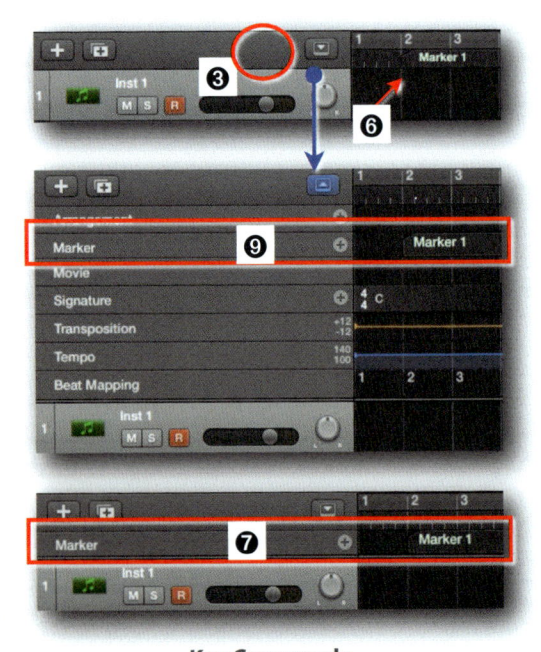

18   2 - Hidden Features

Indication for the First of Multiple Selected Tracks

➡ *Review*

One major improvement in LPX is the ability to select multiple Tracks in the Tracks Window by *sh+clicking* on the Track Header (any contiguous Tracks) or by *cmd+clicking* on the Track Header (any non-contiguous Tracks). Now you can move or delete multiple Tracks at once.

➡ *Attention*

Sometimes, however, you have to know which Track you've selected first. How do you know?

💡 **First Selected Track Indication**

The Track List in the Tracks Window indicates which Track you've selected first in a group of multiple selected Tracks. Unfortunately, this indication is only visible in a specific Track Header Configuration (*ctr+T*):

▸ **Visible**: If you show the *Track Numbers* but not the *Color Bars* ❶, then you can see all the Track Headers highlighted (selected), but only one Track Number ❷ is highlighted. This is the Track that you've selected first.

▸ **Not visible**: If you have the *Track Numbers* ❸ hidden or have the *Color Bars* ❹ shown, then you won't see that indication of the first selected Track.

💡 **When does it matter?**

In same cases it does matter which one was the first one in a group of selected Tracks:

▸ When you add a new Track, then Logic adds the new Track(s) below the selected Track. If multiple Tracks are selected, then it will be below the first selected Track.

▸ If you edit MIDI Regions in the Piano Roll Editor and chose from the local menu *View ➤ One Track* ❺, then the Piano Roll Editor will display all the MIDI Regions of the selected Track. With multiple selected Tracks, it will be the first selected Track and you better know which one that is.

Please note that selecting multiple Tracks will also select all the corresponding Channel Strips in the Mixer, but not the other way around. Selecting multiple Channel Strips in the Mixer Window will select only the first corresponding Track in the Tracks Window.

Show/Hide "Output Track" vs. "Master Track"

➡ Review

The Track Menu in Logic contains the command "*Show/Hide Output Track*" ❶. It has a Key Command assigned to it **sh+cmd+M** ❷, but if we look up that command in the Key Commands Window, we see that the name of the command is different. It is "*Show/Hide Master Track*" ❸. On top of that, under some circumstances, the command in Logic's Track Menu can change to "Show/Hide Master Track ❹. What is going on here?

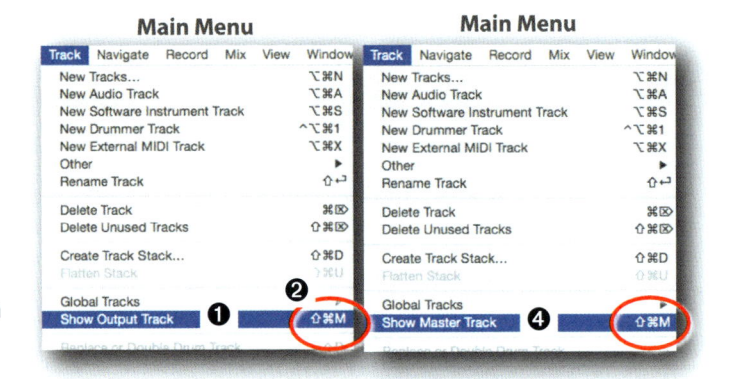

➡ Attention

To shed some light on this confusion, we have to dig a little deeper to make sure we understand some basic concepts in Logic Pro X.

💡 Stereo Project vs Surround Sound Project

There is no single switch that changes a Logic Project to a Surround Sound Project. Once you set the Output Button on one Channel Strip to Surround, then the Logic Project changes to Surround Mode. You won't see any dramatic difference on the outside, but there are a few changes, and one of them is affecting that Menu Command.

▸ Project in Stereo Mode
- **Channel Strip** (Instrument, Audio, Aux): The default output routing in a Logic Project is Stereo. That means, that the Output Buttons on those Channel Strips are set to "Stereo Output" ❺ (or to "None").
- **Output Channel Strip** ❻: This Channel Strip is the representation of the stereo output channels of your connected Audio Interface.
- **Master Channel Strip** ❼: This Channel Strip functions as a VCA Master Fader for the Output Channel Strip(s), and besides the Dim Button 🟧, there is not much use for it.

▸ Project in Surround Mode
- **Channel Strip** (Instrument, Audio, Aux): If you set the Output Button on any of those Channels to Surround ❽, then your Project will change to a Surround Sound Project. This functions as a de-facto Project Surround switch.
- **Output Channel Strip**: Although the Output Channel Strips are the ones that the signal is still routed to (1-6), they might be hidden in the Mixer when the Mixer View is set to "Track". Please note that Audio FX slots are not available on the Output Channel Strips anymore in Surround Mode.
- **Master Channel Strip** ❾: This Channel Strip still functions as a Master VCA Fader for the Output Channel Strip(s), but now has a much more important role, controlling the multiple output channels. In addition, once the Project is switched to Surround, the Audio FX Plugins, the Meters, and the Bounce Button are now added to the Channels Strip.

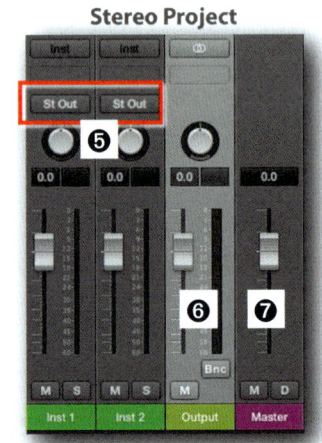

20   2 - Hidden Features

💀 Mysterious Menu Command

Now with that little background, let's look at the menu command again:

▶ **Stereo Mode**
- In Stereo Mode, the Menu Command is "Show/Hide Output Track" ❶.
- It toggles the visibility of a Track ❷ that is assigned to the Output Channel Strip.
- *Ctrl+click* on the Output Channel Strip in the Mixer and use the "Create Track" ❸ command (or its Key Command *ctr+T*) to also add the Track to the Tracks List. You can remove the Track again with the "Show/Hide Output Track" ❶ command.
- The displayed Track is "hard wired" to the Output Channel Strip ❹ and cannot be reassigned to any other Channel Strip. The "Reassign Track" command is missing in the Shortcut Menu when *ctr+clicking* on its Track Header.
- You can use the Create Track Command to add a Track assigned to the Master Channel Strip if you want.

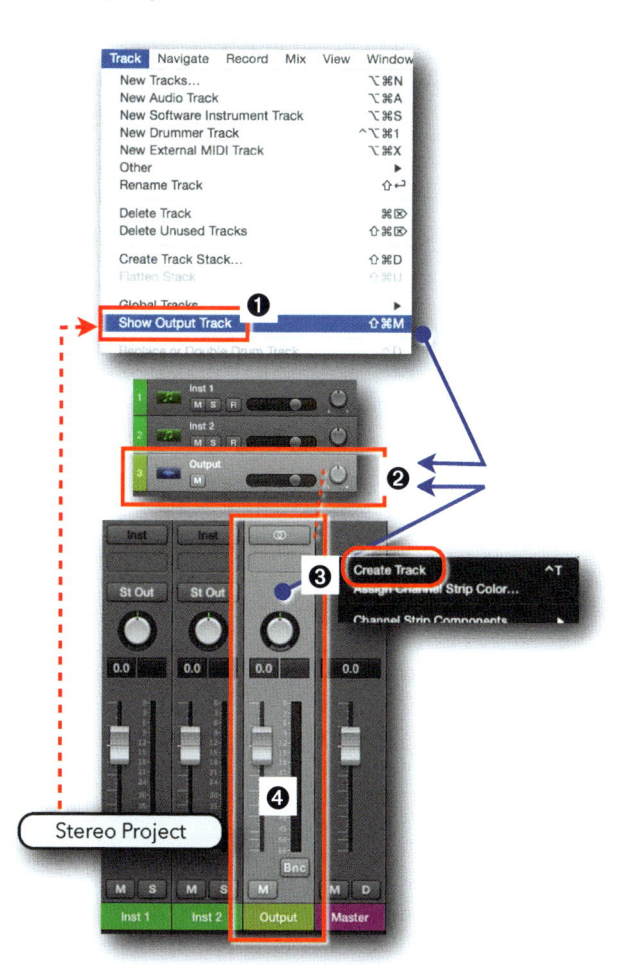

▶ **Surround Mode**
- In Surround Mode, the Menu Command is "Show/Hide Master Track" ❺.
- It toggles the visibility of a Track ❻ that is assigned to the Master Channel Strip.
- *Ctrl+click* on the Master Channel Strip in the Mixer and use the "Create Track" ❼ command (or its Key Command *ctr+T*, to also add the Track to the Tracks List. You can remove the Track again with the "Show/Hide Master Track" command.
- The displayed Track is also "hard wired" to the Master Channel Strip ❽ and cannot be reassigned to any other Channel Strip. The "Reassign Track" command is missing in the Shortcut Menu when *ctr+clicking* on its Track Header.
- Once the Track is visible, it changes between Output Track and Master Track when you switch between Stereo and Surround.

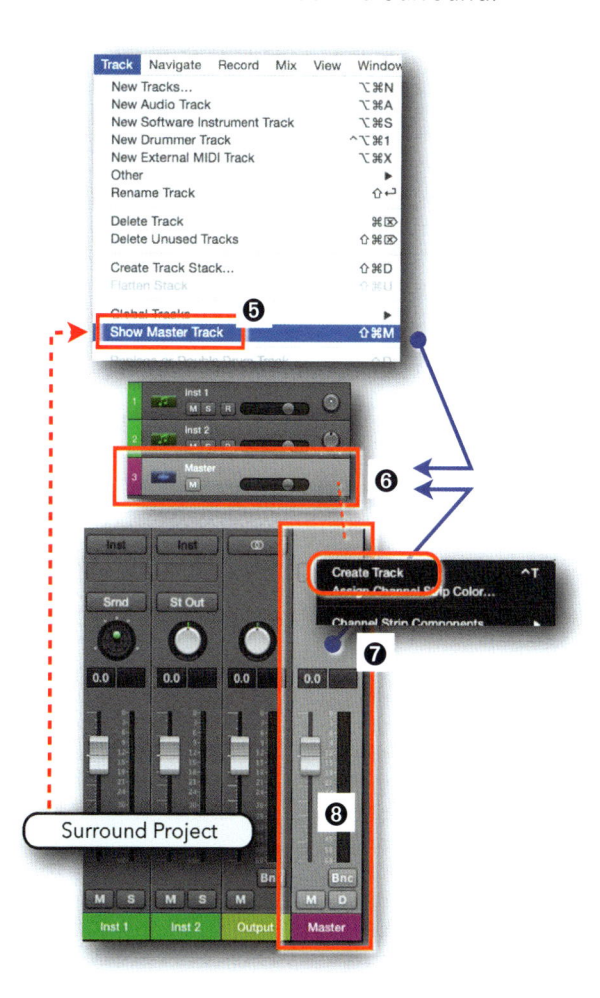

2 - Hidden Features

Capture Recording for Audio Tracks

➡ Review

Capture Recording is an offline recording feature for MIDI data, very simple and easy to use. Think of it this way, Logic is always "listening", it always records the incoming MIDI signal on any record enabled Track in the background. Now instead of clicking the Record Button before you play your part, you can play your part and then hit the "Capture Recording" button ❶ after you played. Logic will then put a Region on the Track Lane with the part you just played on your MIDI controller.

However, Capture Recording only works for MIDI recording and not for audio recording. So, when the vocalist performs his/her best take and you realize that you didn't press record, you are out of luck, or are you?

➡ Attention

When you are playing back your Project with a record-enabled Audio Track and forget to hit the Record Button, you can still capture the current performance when you met the following conditions:

- ☑ Enable the Menu Command *Record ➤ Allow Quick-Punch-In* ❷.
- ☑ Record Enable the Audio Track (not just select the Track, click the Record Enable Button R so it blinks).
- ☑ You must hit the Record Button any time before you stop the playback.
- ☑ Optional, enable the "Record/Record Toggle" Mode if you want to punch-in/punch-out multiple times during the playback.

● Background Recording Procedure

Here is an example of what happens in the background:

- ▶ You start to play at the beginning ❹ of your Project, and at bar 30, you press Record ❺ until bar 45. The new Audio Region ❻ is created from bar 30-45. 
- ▶ When you look at the Project Audio Browser, you will see that Region as a blue section ❼ on the waveform.
- ▶ However, the waveform is much longer, containing a long gray section ❽ prior to where you hit Record. This is the section from hitting the Play Button ❹ until you hit the Record Button ❺. This is what Logic recorded "in the background".
- ▶ On the Track Lane (or in the Project Audio Browser), you can drag the left border ❾ of the Audio Region towards the left to "reveal" that background recording ❿.

22   2 - Hidden Features

Movie File's Embedded Audio Track Plays through System Audio

➡ **Review**

When importing a movie file into your Project, you have to pay attention to the routing of the audio track:

- ▸ A movie file usually has two so-called "tracks" embedded, the video track that contains the picture component and the audio track that contains the sound component. The QuickTime Player app can display those properties ❶.
- ▸ When you import a movie file into your Logic Project, the "Drop Movie" Dialog pops up, where you can select ❷ to import the Video Track ("*Open the movie*") and/or the Audio Track ("*Extract the audio track*").

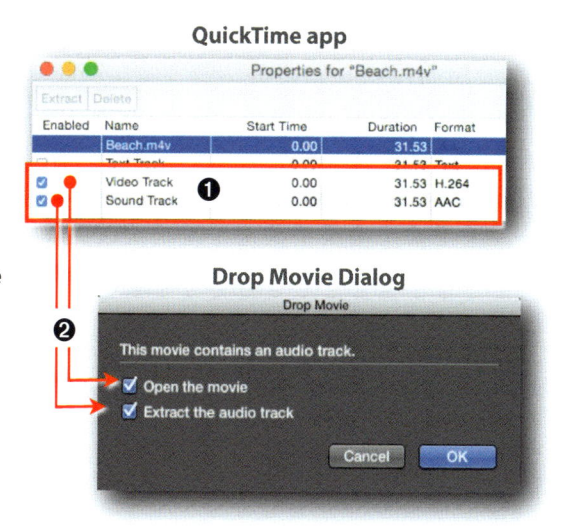

➡ **Attention**

You can use two possible sources for a movie's audio track. Pay attention to their difference.

🎱 **Play Extracted Audio File**

If you chose to extract the audio track from the movie file, then Logic will create a new Audio File ❸ inside the Project file that is represented by the Audio Region ❹ on the newly created Audio Track on top of the Track List of your Project. That Audio Region plays like any other Audio Region in your Project through the Mixer to the selected Audio Device in Logic's *Preferences* ➤ *Audio* ➤ *Devices* ❺.

🎱 **Play Movie File's Embedded Audio Track**

Logic can also play back the embedded audio track directly from the movie file ❻. The *Project Settings* ➤ *Movie* contains a Volume Slider and Mute Button ❼ that controls its level. But here is the important part. That audio track is not played through Logic ❺. It is played directly through the Audio Device ❽, selected in the *System Preferences* ➤ *Sound* ❾.

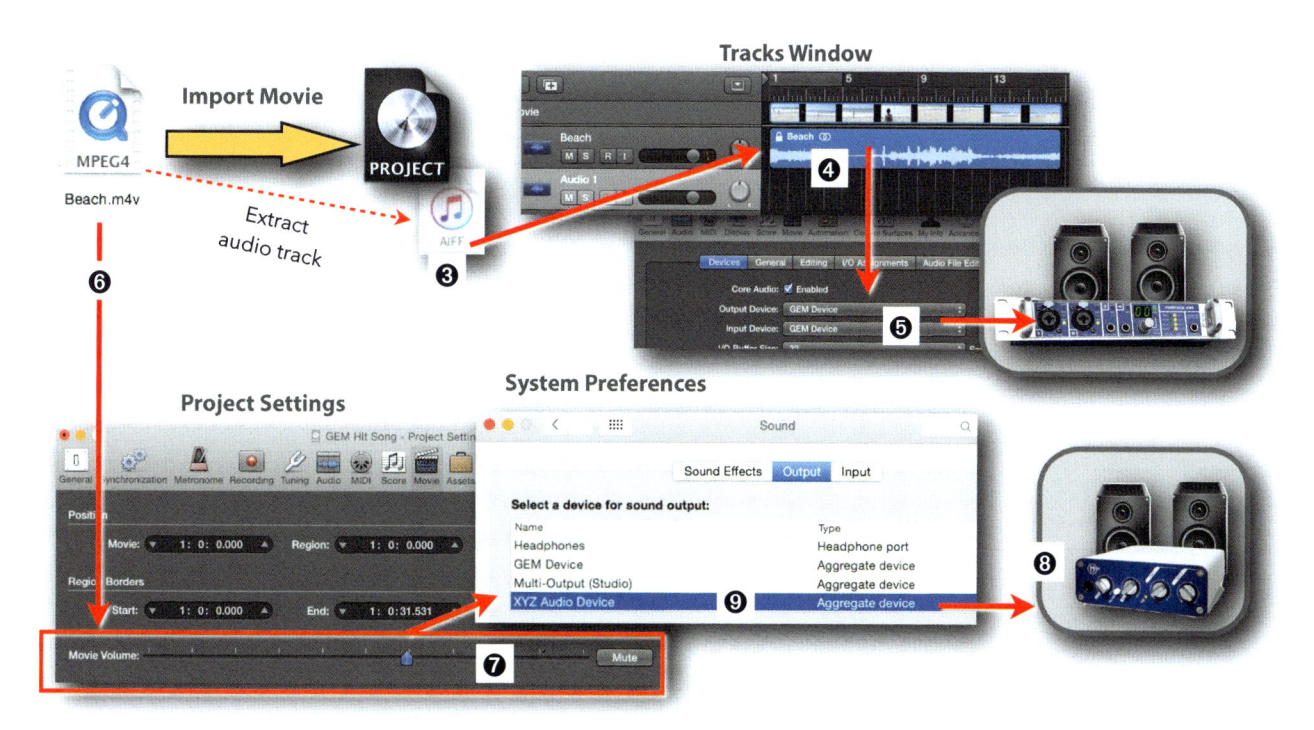

Color Palette Can Display Multiple Selected Colors

→ **Review**

Assigning a color to a Region is as easy as selecting the Region and then *clicking* on a color in the Color Palette Window (*opt+C*). But the Color Palette has an additional feature.

→ **Attention**

When a Region is selected and the Color Palette is open, then it will indicate the color of the selected Region with a frame around that color.

In addition, if you have multiple Regions selected and they have different colors, then the Color Palette will indicate all those colors.

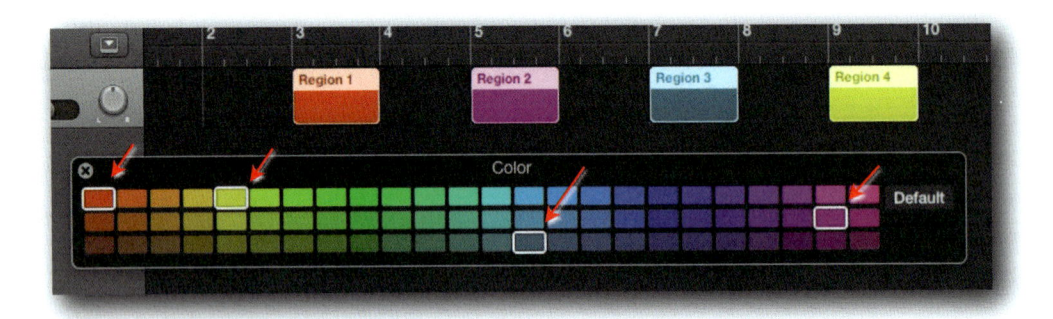

Copy-Paste Graphics from Clipboard to the Track Icon Window

→ **Review**

Ctr+click on the Track Icon in the Track Header ❶ to open the Icon Window, here you can select a Track Icon for that Track. Logic v10.2 added the ability to add Custom Track Icons. Select the Custom Icons ❷ in the sidebar and you can add your own graphics file(s) from the Finder onto the Custom Icons Window ❸ or even directly onto the Track Header ❶. But there is another method.

→ **Attention**

You can copy any image from any app onto the clipboard (*cmd+C*), or take a screenshot, and paste that image directly onto the Custom Icon Window ❸. You have to options:

- When the Custom Icon Window is visible, use the Paste command *cmd+V*
- *Ctr+click* on the Custom Icon Window to open its Shortcut Menu with a single command, *"Paste Icon from Clipboard"* ❹. *Click* on it and the image on the clipboard will be added to the Custom Icons Window.

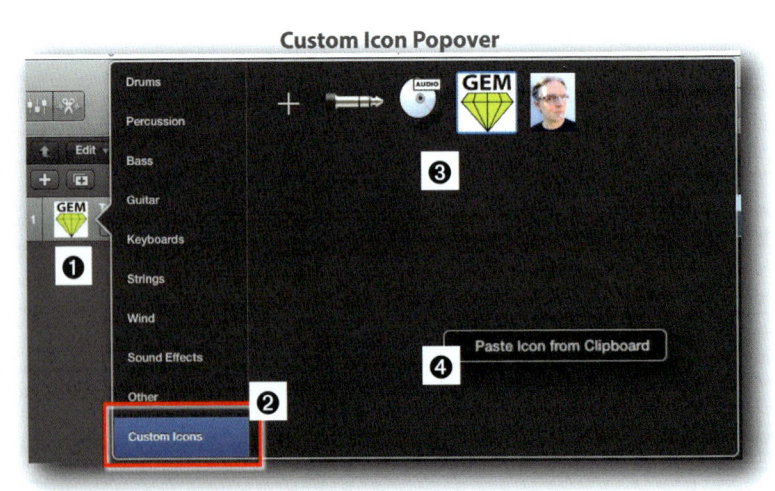

24   2 - Hidden Features

Mixer

Three Different Input Monitoring Buttons

➡ **Review**

The appearance and functionality of the Input Monitoring Button on the Track Header and Channel Strip can be confusing, especially with the Preferences settings *Preferences ➤ Audio ➤ General ➤ "Input monitoring only for focused track, and record-enabled tracks"* ❶.

In the Logic User Guide and various Logic books the functionality is often explained incorrectly or over-simplified.

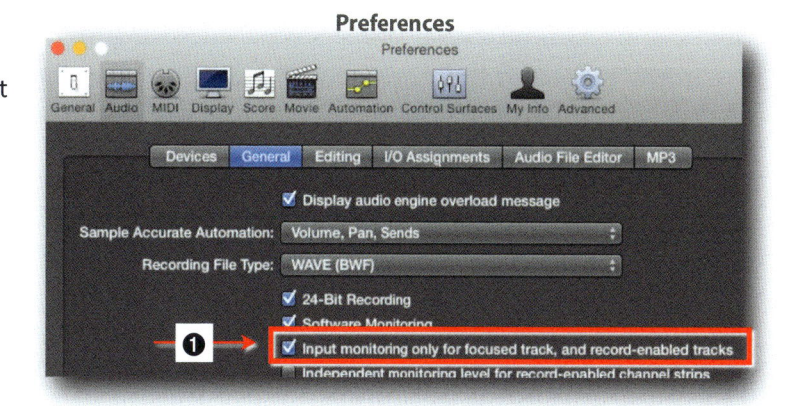

➡ **Attention**

You have to pay attention to the appearance of the Input Monitoring Button. It can have three different colors on the Track Header, but only two on the Channel Strip.

☐ Input monitoring only for focused track, and record-enabled tracks

When un-checked, the behavior is like in Logic Pro 9:

- **Input Monitoring Off**: You won't hear the incoming signal on that Track (unless you record-enable the Track R).
- **Input Monitoring On**: You will hear the incoming signal. You can even enable the Input Monitoring Button on multiple Tracks ❷ to listen to all those incoming signals, even if they're coming from the same input channel.

☑ Input monitoring only for focused track, and record-enabled tracks

This is the new behavior in LPX. The checkbox is enabled by default, so make sure to understand the implications (also on the next pages):

- Even if you have Input Monitoring enabled on multiple Tracks, only the selected Track ❸ (focused track) will have the Input Monitoring enabled. The Input Monitoring Button could be off and Input Monitoring could still be activated, if the Track is selected.
- Any other Track that had the Input Monitoring Button enabled switches the button to that special off status ❹. It means, "technically I'm enabled, but I was overwritten and disabled because my Track is not selected (or record enabled)". The button on the Channel Strip remains in this status.
- There is one exception: When you record-enable R an unselected Track, then it will turn monitoring on, displaying this button combination R ❺.

2 - Hidden Features

Level Meter Reads Audio Input When Record-Enabled

➡ Review

To properly use any meter or gauge, you not only need to know **what** the displayed value is, but also **where** the value was measured. For example, if the dashboard of a car displays a temperature value of 30°C, then you also need to know whether that value was measured inside the car, outside the car, or at the engine, otherwise, you cannot do much with that information. The same thing is true for any type of meters in Logic, especially the Level Meter on the Channel Strip and Track Header (which show the same reading).

Logic has a command ❶ that lets you toggle the Pre-Fader Metering. This implies that the meter can read the audio signal at two points along the signal flow of a Channel Strip, either before or after the Volume Fader. However, there is a third "reading point" and a lot of conditions and circumstances to be aware of.

➡ Attention

Although the on-off status of the Pre-Fader Metering implies two points along the signal flow where the meter measures the audio signal level, there are actually three points. Here is a simplified signal flow diagram of Logic's Audio Channel Strip that shows the details.

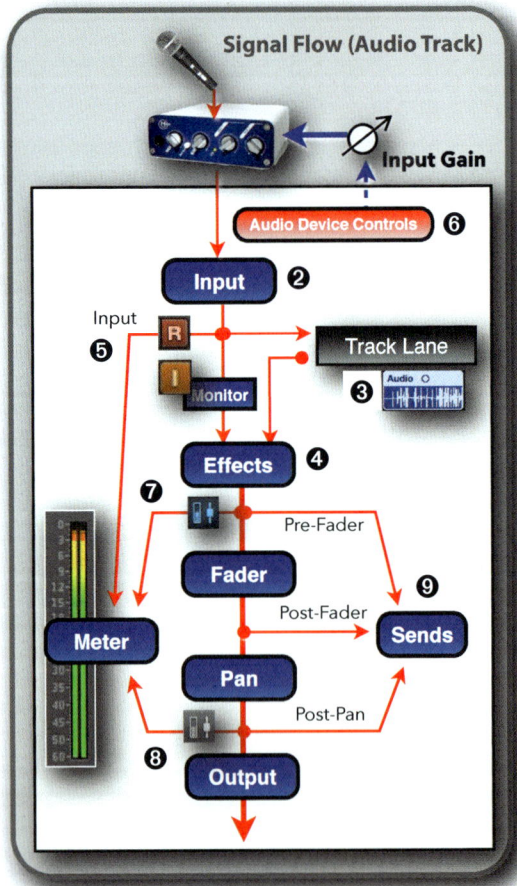

💡 Pre-Effects

This is an important measuring point, because it reads the actual Input signal ❷, how it will be recorded onto a Track ❸ as an Audio Region. If you were to measure after the Effects ❹ (which often alter the level), then you would not know the exact level of the audio signal you are recording in Logic ❸.

Any time you record-enable a Track, you actually switch the Level Meter ❺ to read the Input signal regardless of the Pre-Fader Button. Now with the *Audio Device Controls* knob ❻ on a Channel Strip, you can adjust that Input level by remotely setting the input gain on the external audio interface with that knob.

💡 Pre-Fader

This measuring point ❼ reads the audio signal before the Fader, but after the Effects. It is the same level that you send to a Pre-Fader Aux Send ❾ (but after the Mute Button!).

💡 Post-Fader

This measuring point ❽ reads the signal after the Fader, but after the Pan Control. It is the same level that you send to a Post-Pan Aux Send ❾. BTW, the Aux Sends provide the option of a true Post Fader that is Pre-Pan.

As you can see, keeping an eye (or a mental image) on the Channel Strip's signal flow and knowing what is going through *where* and *when* is very important. Here are the various buttons that might or might not influence that signal flow, so you get an idea of how complex it can be with different button settings to predict anything.

- Status buttons for Input Monitoring
- Software Monitoring
- Auto Input Monitoring
- Pre/Post Fader Metering
- Transport Controls

26   2 - Hidden Features

Here is a look at the signal flow diagram again; this is what it looks like when any of the three Input Monitoring buttons are enabled. Please be aware that you are feeding two signals into the Channel Strip. There is quite a significant difference between those two signals when it comes to metering and monitoring, so follow the signal flow carefully to know what you *see* (Meter) and *hear* (Output Bus).

- ☑ The **Input signal** ❶ is coming from your audio interface. This is what you are about to record.
- ☑ The **Track signal** ❷ is coming from all the Audio Regions on the Track Lane (only when playing back). This is what was recorded already.

Record Enable

These are the conditions when the Record Enable Button is active:

- ▸ Software Monitoring only affects the Input signal. If off ❸, then Effect Plugins are bypassed, and the signal is not routed to the Output, but still visible on the Meter.
- ▸ Auto Input Monitoring only affects the Input signal. It mutes it during Play ❹ but you still can see it on the meter.
- ▸ Per-Fader Metering has no affect.
- ▸ The Track signal, when played back, is not displayed on the Volume Meter at all ❺!

Input Monitoring

These are the conditions when the Input Monitoring Button is active but not the Record Enable Button:

- ▸ Software Monitoring only affects the Input signal depending on the Transport Controls ❻:
  - • Plugins are bypassed, and the signal is not routed to the Output, but visible on the Meter.
  - • No Input signal at the Meter or Output at all.
- ▸ Auto Input Monitoring has no effect.

"… only focused tracks …"

These are the (confusing?) conditions when that special checkbox in the Preferences is active ("*Input monitoring only for focused track, and record-enabled tracks*") but not the Input Monitoring Button or the Record Enable Button:

- ▸ Software Monitoring has no effect.
- ▸ Auto Input Monitoring has no effect.
- ▸ There are several conditions for the Input signal:
  - • Input signal is not routed to the Output ❼.
  - • Input signal is not sent to any Aux Send!
  - • Input signal is not routed through the Plugins ❽ in Post Fader Metering.

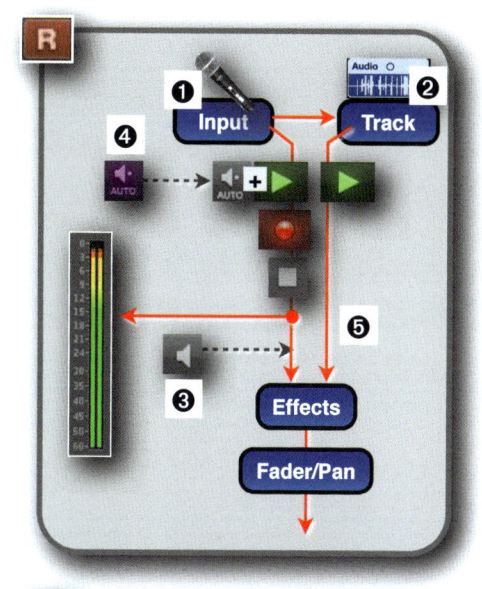

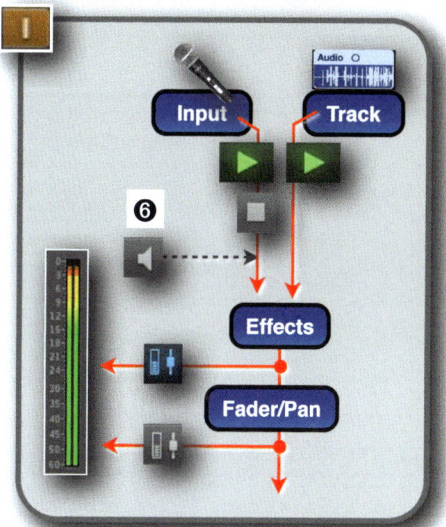

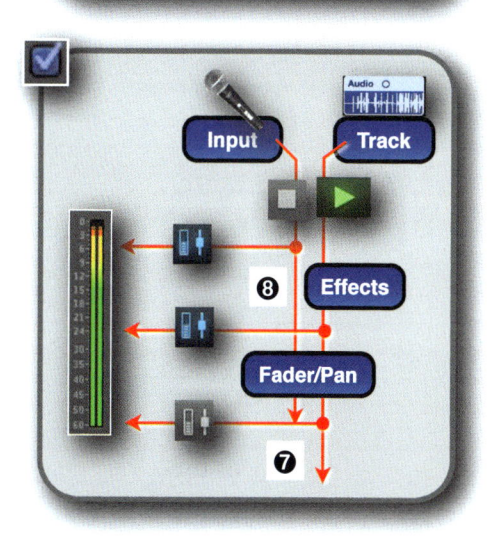

2 - Hidden Features   27

Here are the various combinations shown as a matrix:

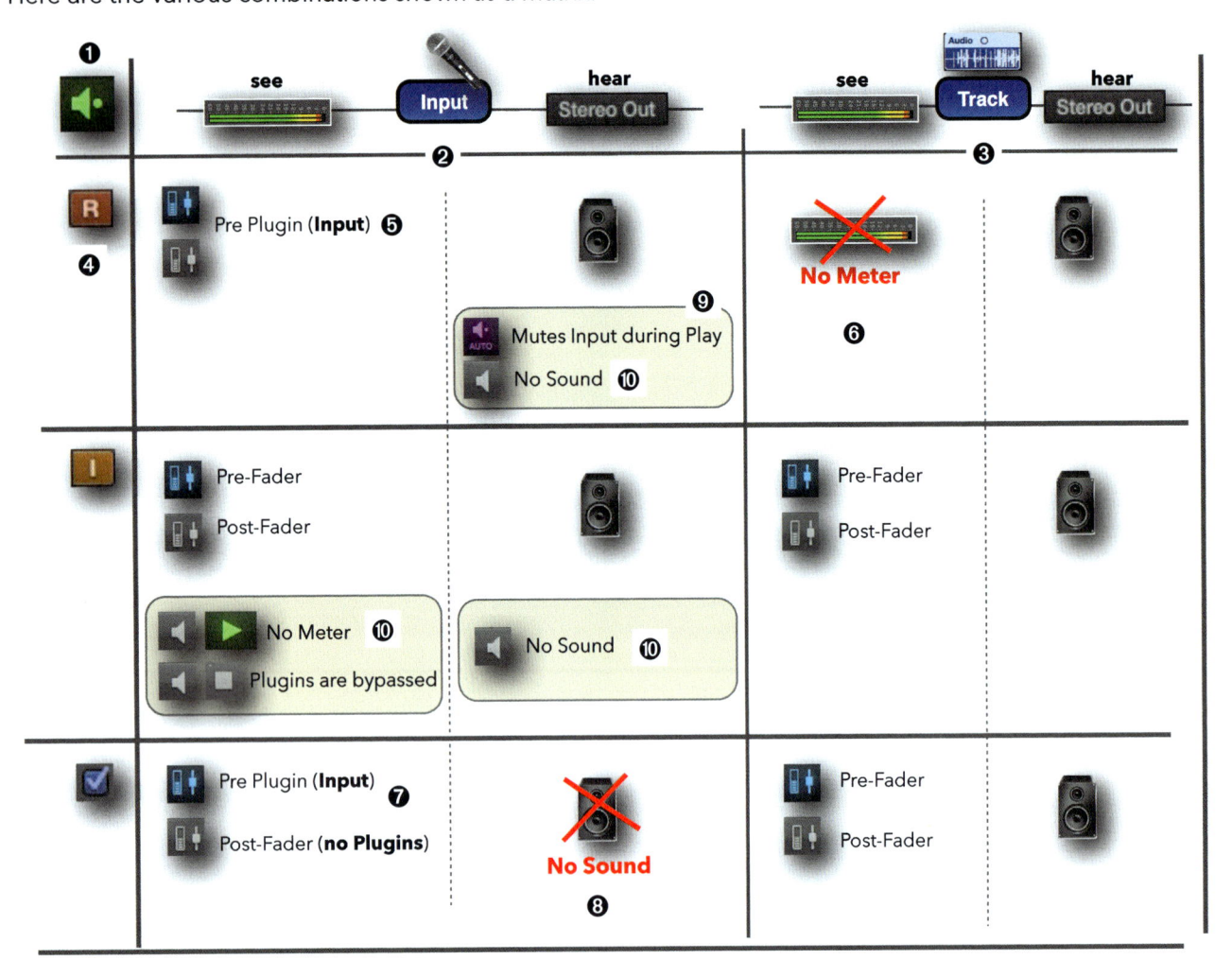

❶ The Matrix shows you the effect when combining all the different buttons when Software Monitoring 🔊 is enabled. There are three scenarios where it has an effect when disabled ❿.

❷ This double column shows you what happens to the Input signal, how you can <u>see</u> it on the Meter and how you can <u>hear</u> it on the Output Bus.

❸ This double column shows you what happens to the Track signal, when playing back its Audio Regions, how you can <u>see</u> the signal on the Meter and how you can <u>hear</u> it on the Output bus.

❹ The three rows show you what happens when you enable the Record Enable Button R, the Input Monitoring Button I, or the checkbox ☑ in the **Preferences ➤ Audio ➤ General ➤ Input Monitoring only for focused tracks and Record enabled tracks**. If a combination of any of those three buttons are selected, then the priority is R over I over ☑.

❺ The Meter ignores the Pre-Fader Metering Button and shows the Input signal before the Effect Plugins, the unprocessed Input signal as it will be recorded to an Audio Region.

❻ If the Record Enable Button R is active, then the Track signal will not be displayed on the Meters during playback!

❼ If the Pre-Fader Metering Button is enabled, then the Meter will actually show the Input signal before the Effect Plugins. If it is not selected, then it will display the signal after the Fader, but with Plugins disabled.

❽ The Input signal will be displayed on the Meter, but it is not routed to the Output Bus.

❾ The Auto Input Monitoring Button has only one effect. The Input signal is muted on the Output Bus during Playback ▶ when Record Enable is selected R.

❿ There are a few "consequences" for the Input signal when you disable Software Monitoring 🔊.

28 2 - Hidden Features

Input Monitoring Automatically Lowers Fader for Internal Microphone

➡ Review

Recording with a microphone that is close by the speakers creates one potential problem: Feedback. Logic is kind of feedback-aware with the following mechanism.

➡ Attention

As we have seen in the previous section, when you enable the Input Monitoring Button, the audio signal that you feed into the Channel Strip will be routed through its outputs so you can listen back to it (monitor). This is exactly the dangerous setup for a feedback loop. You will have that situation, for example, when you use the built-in microphone on your computer and listen back with your built-in speakers. The microphone and the speakers are very close in distance to each other, and if you have the speaker volume turned up, then you will hear feedback when you enable Input Monitoring.

⦿ Avoid Feedback

Logic is aware of such situation and acts accordingly.

- Let's say you have the Built-in Microphone ❶ selected as the Input Device in Logic's Preferences.
- And, let's say you select that Input on an Audio Channel Strip ❷.
- Now when you enable the Input Monitoring Button ❸ on that Channel Strip, the following will happen:
    - ☑ The Volume Fader ❹ automatically is lowered to -24dB to avoid the feedback.
    - ☑ A Dialog Window pops up ❺, warning you about the potential feedback. You can acknowledge that by *clicking* the OK Button, or *click* the "Choose Audio Device…" button. This will open the Audio Preferences window ❶ in Logic where you can select a different Input Device.

Please note that the Volume Level doesn't move back to its previous level when you disable the Input Monitoring Button. You have to do it manually.

Also, the interesting thing is that selecting the Record Enable Button will not lower the Volume Fader, even if that has the same feedback potential (listening to the input signal).

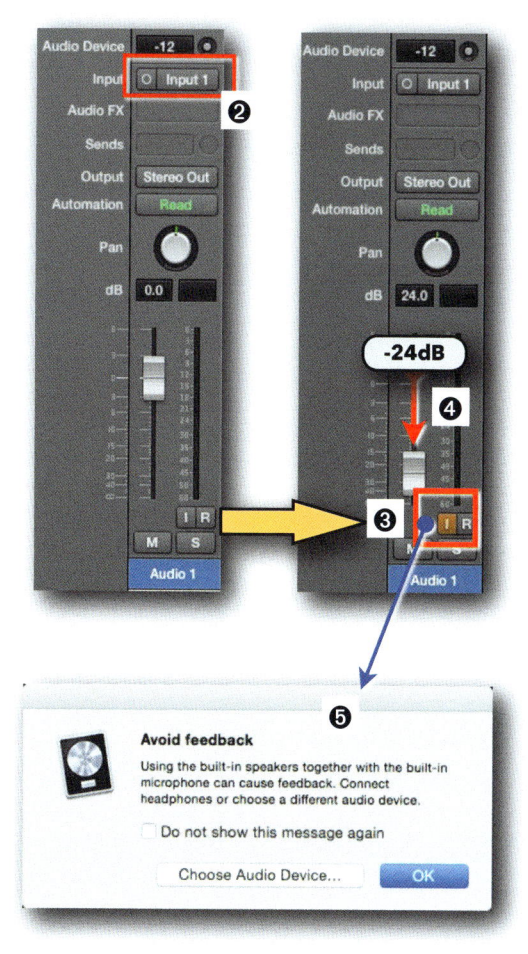

Play through Multiple Audio Devices Simultaneously

➡ *Review*

Logic only allows you to select one audio device to use for your audio outputs and one device for your audio inputs, so you have to choose which interface to select in Logic. However, the Audio MIDI Setup utility (*/Applications/Utilities/*) lets you create two different types of so-called *virtual audio devices*, **Aggregate Devices** and **Multi-Output Devices**, that circumvents that imitation. Aggregate Devices have already been around for many years and are used mainly by advanced Logic users, but the newer Multi-Output Device (added in OSX 10.7) provides a functionality that can be used even in smaller home studio setups.

➡ *Attention*

Aggregate Device: This device lets you combine multiple audio devices to access their combined inputs and outputs. That means, you can route the output of a Channel Strip to any output of those audio devices in that group or record from any input from those devices.

Multi-Output Device: This device only lets you combine the outputs of multiple audio devices, but it has the advantage that the output of a Channel Strip is routed simultaneously to the outputs of all those devices in that group.

Here is an example of how you can use such a Multi-Output Device:

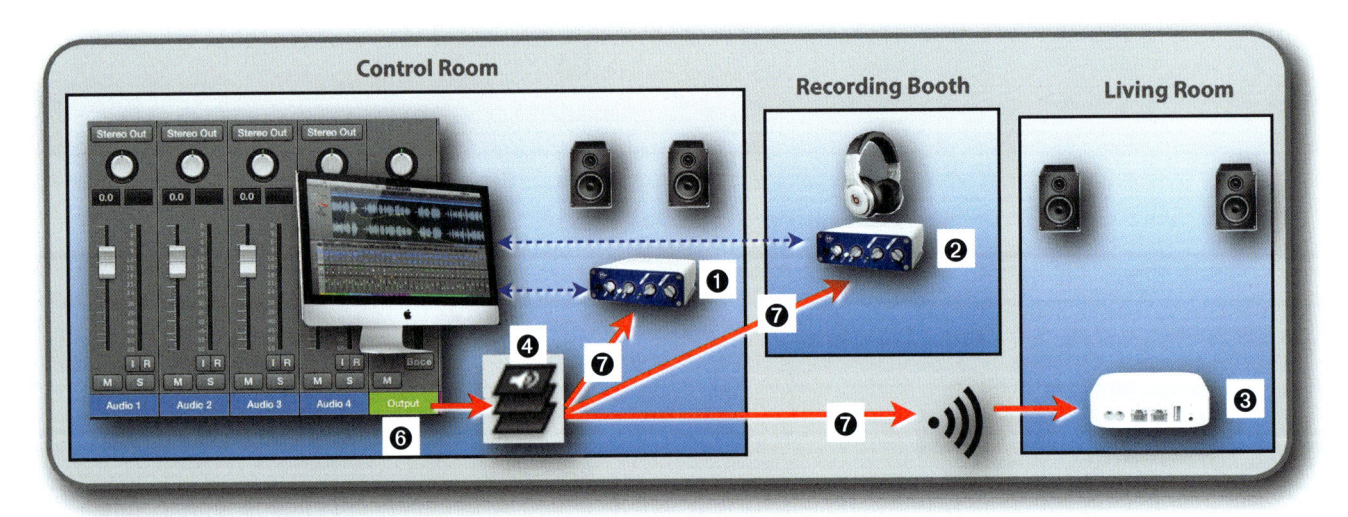

- One Audio Interface (A) is hooked up to your studio monitors in the control room ❶.
- One Audio Interface (B) is hooked up to the headphone system in your recording booth ❷.
- You use an Airport Express (C) that is hooked up to your speakers in your living room ❸.
- In the Audio MIDI Setup utility you can define a Multi-Output Device ❹ that contains all three Audio Interfaces (A, B, C).
- When you select the Multi-Output Device in Logic's Preferences ❺, the output of your mix ❻ is sent to all three Audio Interfaces playing your mix simultaneously ❼ on all speakers/headphones.

💡 Setup

The configuration and setup of a Multi-Output Device is done in the Audio MIDI Setup ❶ utility, located in the */Applications/Utilities* directory, where you open the Audio Devices window (***cmd+2***). As a default, the Audio MIDI Setup utility already contains one Multi-Output Device 🗂 (and one Aggregate Device ➕). You can create multiple of those devices with different configurations.

- ▸ **Create** more Multi-Output Devices by *clicking* the Plus button in the lower left corner and select "Create Multi-Output Device"❷.
- ▸ **Rename** a device by *double-clicking* on it and typing in a name.
- ▸ Select the Multi-Output Device in the Device List ❸ on the left and it will display all the available devices on the right.
- ▸ ☑ **Use**: Enable the checkbox in the Use column ❹ for each device that you want to include in that virtual device. These will be the devices that will receive the output signal from Logic if you select this Multi-Output Device as Logic's Output Device ❺. The disclosure triangle ❻, next to the Multi-Output Device icon, lets you reveal the list of all the Audio Devices that are used in that virtual device.

- ▸ 🕒 **Master Device/Sample Rate**: From the popup menu at the top ❼, select the Device that should provide the master clock for that group of devices. The second popup menu lets you choose the Sample Rate on that Device (if available). The clock icon ❽ in the Devices List indicates which audio device in that group functions as the master.

- ▸ 〰️ **Drift Correction (Re-sampling)**: Any Device in the group that is not connected via a Word Clock to the selected Master Device needs to be re-sampled to guarantee the proper synchronization of their digital audio signals. *Click* the Drift Correction ❾ checkbox to enable that. The waveform icon ❽ on the left indicates which audio device in that group will be resampled.

    The audio signals of non-synchronized audio devices will drift, which causes degradation of the audio quality and nasty clicks. I provide an in-depth explanation with lots of background information for that topic in the "Synchronization" chapter of my book "Logic Pro X - The Details".

- ▸ *Right-click* on a device or use the Action Button (gear icon) to open a Shortcut Menu ❿ with more commands.

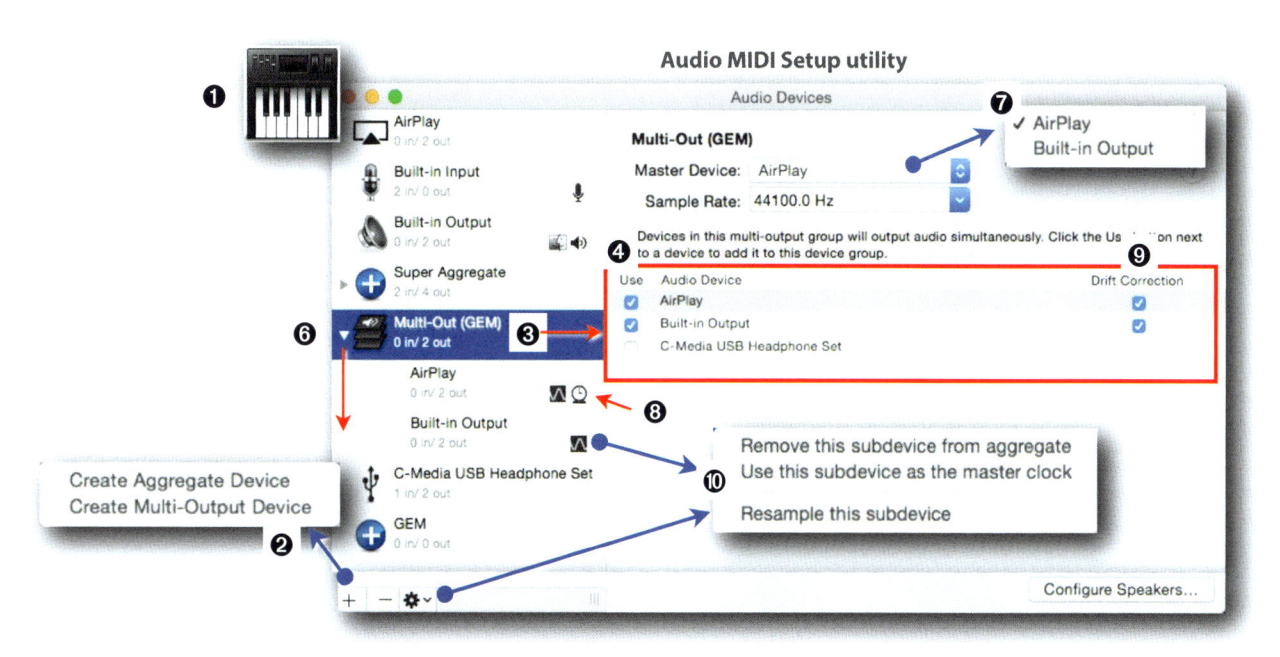

2 - Hidden Features

"Show Only" a Specific Channel Strip Group

Key Commands Window

➡ **Review**

There are nine powerful Key Commands ❶ that affect the functionality of the Channel Strip Groups. They are labeled "*Toggle Hide Group 1*" … "*Toggle Hide Group 9*" and are assigned to the key combination **sh+ctr+1** to **sh+ctr+9**. They correspond to the checkbox in the Group Inspector, next to each Group ❷.

➡ **Attention**

You have to look closely at the example I provided here and reproduce it to fully understand its hidden power.

🔘 **Setup**

- Assign each Channel Strip to Channel Strip Group 1
- Assign an additional Group Number to those Channel Strips that you would like to group together. For example Drums, Vocals, Guitars, etc.
- Now all those Channel Strips have an assignment like 1+2, 1+3, 1+4, etc. ❸.

🔘 **Functionality**

Now, here are two (!) ways to use those groups:

▶ **Hide only**: If you use any of the Key Commands, you can toggle the visibility of a specific Group. For example, using the Key Command **sh+ctr+2** will show/hide those Channel Strips assigned to Group 2 ❹.

▶ **Show only**: With the following trick, you can use the Key Command to show only the Channel Strips that belong to a specific Group:

  - First, use the Key Command to Hide Group 1. All the Channel Strips belonging to that group are now hidden ❺.
  - Now when in this state, if you use any other Key Command, for example "*Toggle Hide Group 2*", it will "un-hide" only those Channel Strips ❻. Because Group 2 was hidden (due to the fact that they also belong to Group 1), the Key Command toggles the visibility and now shows those Channels again. Try it out to understand it.

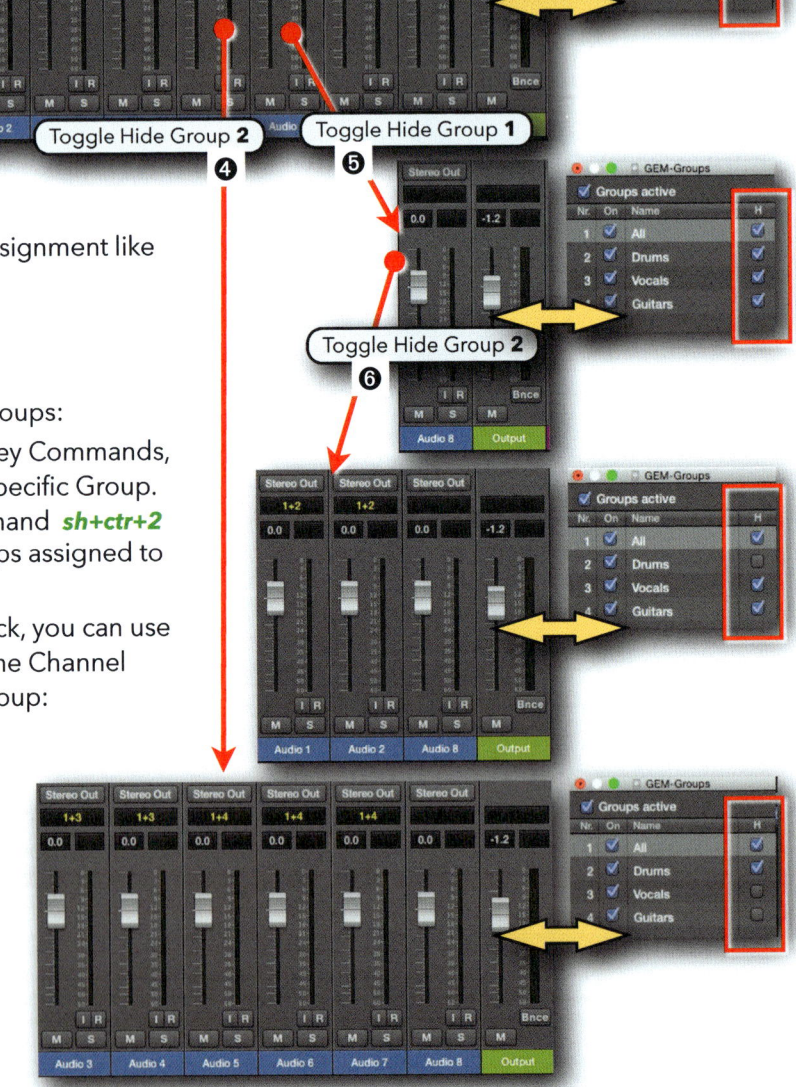

32   2 - Hidden Features

Stereo vs. Two Mono Output Channel Strips

➡ **Review**

There are different variations of the Input Button on a Channel Strip.

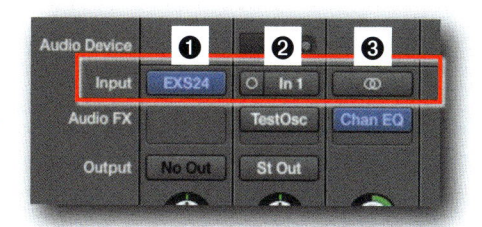

❶ For an Instrument Channel Strip the Input Button functions as the Instrument Plugin Slot where you select the Software Instrument as the Channel Strip's sound source.

❷ The Audio Channel Strips and Aux Channel Strips have a double button that lets you select the input source on the right and the input format (mono, stereo, etc.) on the left when you move over the button.

❸ The Output Channel Strip just has the Input Format Button and that has a special functionality you have to be aware of.

➡ **Attention**

Clicking on the Input Format Button ❹ of the Output Channel Strip will change the single stereo Output Channel Strip ❺ to two mono Output Channel Strips ❻ and its Input Format Button changes to the mono symbol ❼ to indicate that. *Clicking* on the Format Button ❼ of any of the now two Output Channel Strips will change them back to a single stereo Output Channel Strip ❺. Let's see what is going on:

The left and right output busses (output channels) ❽ are routed through a single stereo Output Channel Strip.

The left and right output busses (output channels) ❾ are routed through two separate mono Output Channel Strips.

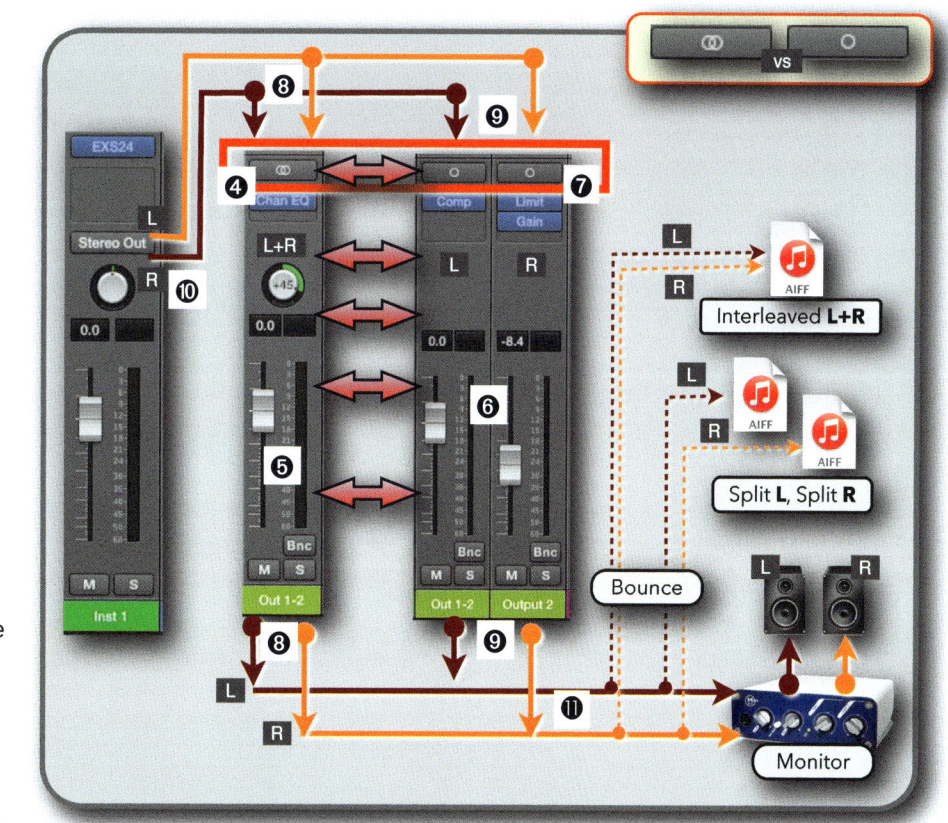

▸ Nothing changes for Channel Strips that route their signal to the stereo output busses ❿.

▸ Nothing changes after the Output Channel Strips ⓫. There are still two channels (busses L+R), that are sent to the audio interface to listen to the left and right speaker and the two channels (busses) that create the interleaved stereo file or the two split mono files.

▸ However, the stereo ❺ and the two mono ❻ Channel Strips are independent "Environment" objects. That means independent Channel Strip components like Volume, Plugins, etc.

2 - Hidden Features   33

Bounce individual Mono Files

One hidden advantage of this stereo vs mono Output Channel Strip is the option to bounce a single mono channel. If you look closely at the two mono Output Channel Strips, then you can see that they both have their individual Bounce Button ❶. They open a special Bounce Window that has the File Type selector disabled (grayed out) ❷. *Clicking* on the Bounce Button of the left or right Output Channel will only bounce that channel to a single one-channel (mono) audio file. The Bounce Button on a stereo Output Channel Strip opens the Bounce Window with the option to bounce to an interleaved stereo file or two split mono files ❸.

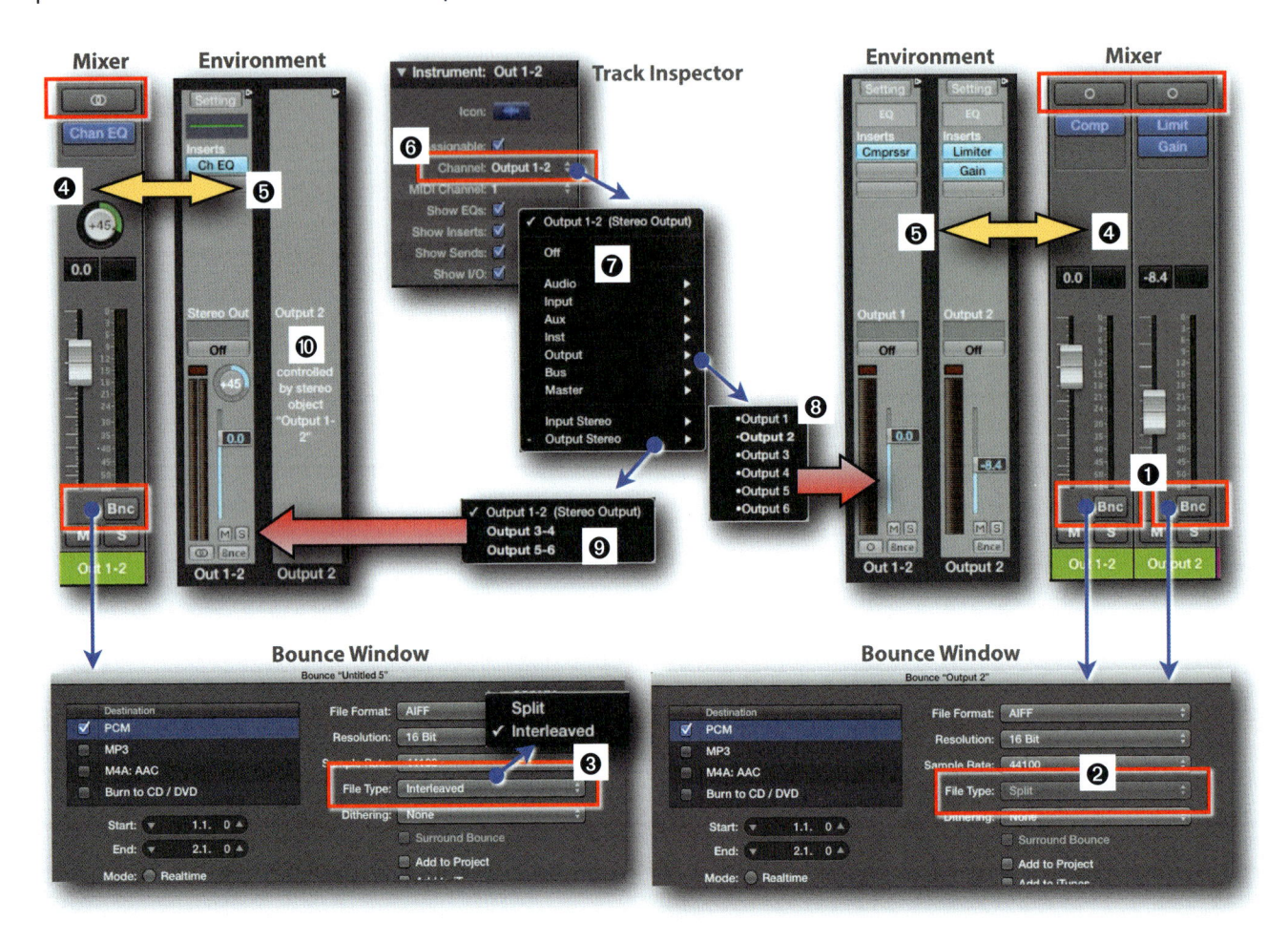

Environment

If you are still following what has happened so far, then let's lift the curtain and peak behind the Environment Window..

- ▶ Each Channel Strip in the Mixer Window ❹ is a (nicer looking) representation of an Environment Object ❺ of the object type "Channel Strip".
- ▶ The Channel Parameter ❻, in the Object Inspector, defines what type of Channel Strip that object will be.
- ▶ This Object Parameter opens a popup menu with all the Channel Strip Types ❼.
- ▶ The Input and Output Channels have two submenus. Selecting one from the upper section defines a mono Channel Strip ❽ and selecting one from the bottom defines the object as a stereo Channel Strip ❾.
- ▶ If the stereo Channel Strip is selected, then the second object (previous Output 2) turns blank with a message explaining why ❿.
- ▶ The objects "remember" their individual settings (Plugins, Volume Fader, etc.) when you switch between stereo and mono. Don' mind the misleading Channel Strip Name "Out 1-2" when switched to mono Channel Strips.

34   2 - Hidden Features

Solo Safe on Output Channel Strip

➡ **Review**

Every Channel Strip has a Solo Button so you can listen to just that one Channel Strip by automatically muting all the other Channel Strips. How about the Output Channel Strip? Does it actually need a Solo Button, and what for? If all the Channel Strips on the Mixer are routed to that Output Channel Strip, isn't a Solo Button kind of redundant? Or maybe it isn't.

➡ **Attention**

Two things to pay attention to:

🔵 Solo Button or not

Maybe you never realized it, but the Output Channel Strip might or might not have a Solo Button [S] at all. It depends on how many channels the currently selected Audio Device has:

- ❶ Audio Device with 2 channels ➤ no Solo Button
- ❷ Audio Device with more than 2 channels ➤ yes Solo Button

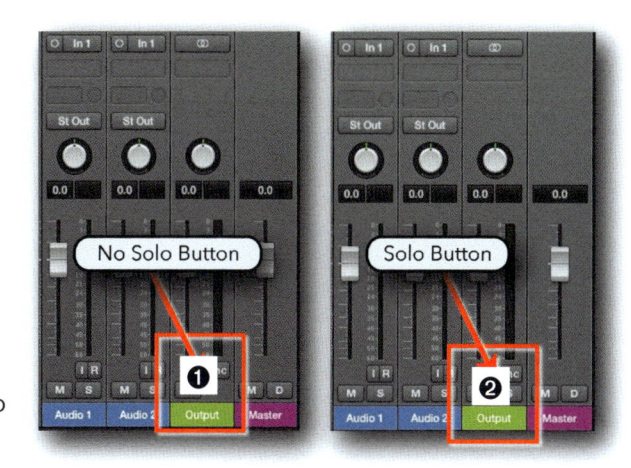

🔵 Output Channel Strip - Solo Safe

Here is a simple mixer setup with two Output Channel Strips to demonstrate the important Solo Safe function on an Output Channel Strip:

- ▶ The Mixer has two Audio Channel Strips. Audio 1 ❸ is routed to Output Channel 1-2 ❺ and Audio 2 ❹ to Output Channel 5-6 ❻.
- ▶ The Master Channel Strip functions as a VCA Master Fader for all the Output Channel Strips, in this case, Output Channel Strip 1-2 ❺ and Output Channel Strip 5-6 ❻. That means, lowering the Volume Fader on the Master Channel Strip ❼ offsets the level on both Output Channel Strips ❽.
- ▶ Setting the Output Channel Strip to Solo Safe ❾ (*ctr+click* on the Solo Button), will have two consequences:
  - Soloing a Channel Strip that is routed to Output Channel 5-6 would mute Output Channel Strip 1-2. When Output 1-2 is set to Solo Safe, it will not be muted.
  - A solo-safe Output Channel Strip ❾ will ignore the level offset sent from the Master Channel Strip. You can see in this example that the level on Output Channel Strip 1-2 did not change ❿.

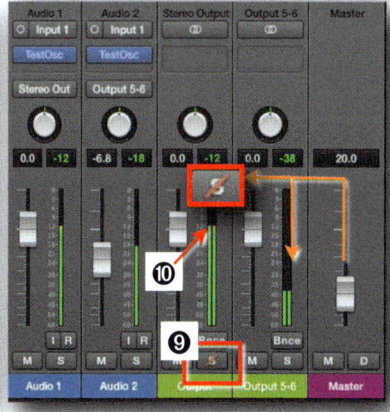

2 - Hidden Features 35

Workflow

Use "Go to Position Window" as Memory Locator

➡ Review

If you want to go to a specific position in your Project, you can simply *click* on that position in the Ruler to move the Playhead there. However, if that position is "out of sight" and you need to scroll there first, or if you want to position the Playhead at a precise position in Musical Time (bars and beats) or Absolute Time (minutes and samples), then you might want to use the "Go to Position" window.

You can open the window ❶ in two ways:
- Main Menu ❷ *Navigate* ➤ *Go To* ➤ *Position ...*
- Key Command (*Go to Position...*) **/**

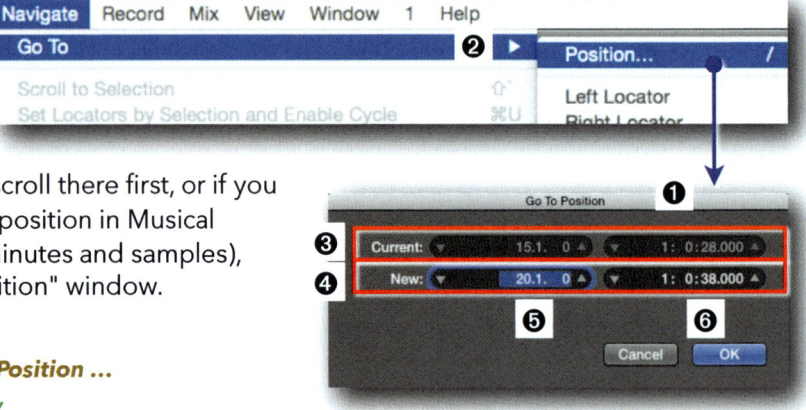

➡ Attention

Here is how the window works and how to use it for an unintended purpose:

💡 Functionality

The window displays four fields:

- **Current ❸**: These two read-only fields show the current position of the Playhead in Musical Time ❺ and Absolute Time ❻.
- **New ❹**: These two fields let you enter a new position as Musical Time or Absolute Time. Entering one time value will update the other time value accordingly.

Closing the window with the OK button will place the Playhead at the New Position.

💡 The Problem

Logic doesn't have Memory Locators like other DAWs or like old-school tape machines. Memory Locators are handy during recording or mixing when you often have to position the Playhead at a specific position (Verse, Chorus, etc.). You store various positions to a memory preset (#1 ... #99) and when you recall such a preset, the Playhead goes to that position.

In Logic, you can only use Markers and the Left/Right Cycle Locator as Memory Locators. However, they are not really suited for such a task, because their position can change depending on various circumstances.

💡 The Solution

You can use the Go To Position Window as a single Memory Locator, because the window remembers the position you entered in the New field. If you have entered bar 5 and later wanted to go back to bar 5, you just hit the forward slash key **/** (the Key Command to open the window), and then right away the *return* key (which will close the window and position the Playhead at bar 5, the value in the New field).

💡 The Bug

Unfortunately, there is a bug in the current 10.2 version of Logic. When you open the *Go to Position* Window, it doesn't remember the last New Position, instead, it displays the Current Position. This is redundant, because that is what the Current Position field already displays. Hopefully, that bug will be fixed in v10.2.1.

List of All Open Windows in the Window Menu

➡ **Review**

Several windows in Logic (Mixer, Piano Roll, Smart Controls, etc.) can be viewed in two ways, Window Panes inside Logic's Main Window and Standalone Windows. The commands to toggle the Window Panes are listed under the View Menu ❶ and the commands to open the Standalone Windows are listed under the Window Menu ❷.

The Window Menu has one section at the bottom ❸ that is dynamic, which means the available commands change. Let's have a closer look at it.

➡ **Attention**

The commands below the "Hide All Plug-in Windows" follow these rules:

🔸 **Open Windows**

Most of the Standalone Windows that are open in Logic are listed here (with the exception of the floating windows like Plugin or the Movie windows). These commands ❸ are helpful, especially when you want to view a window that is hidden by another window. Select a command to open that window to make it the Active Window.

🔸 **Naming Convention**

Those menu commands contain the name of the Project, followed by a hyphen and the name of the window. This way you can differentiate if you have multiple Projects open at one time ❹.

🔸 **Status Indication**

The commands have a symbol ❺ in front of the name to indicate their current status:

✓ This is the window that is currently active in Logic (focused), the one with the red (close) Title Bar Button.

• These are all the Inactive Windows, that don't have key focus.

♦ These are the Inactive Window that are moved to the Dock (with the "Minimize" command).

These are windows that don't "belong" to a specific Project.

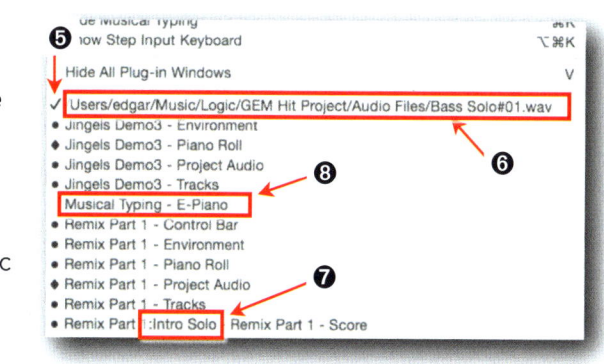

🔸 **Special Window Names**

Some windows have a special naming convention:

❻ The Audio File Editor shows the path name of the audio file it is displaying.

❼ Some Editor Windows display the name of the current Region.

❽ If a window doesn't belong to a specific Project (Keyboard or Musical Typing), then it will only show its name and the name of the currently selected MIDI Track (the recipient of the MIDI notes).

Dock and Mission Control with Logic

➡ Review

The Dock is a very useful feature in OSX. Every app that is currently running is listed in the Dock with a little dot next to it ❶. You can even keep an app icon in the Dock after you quit the app (now listed without a dot) so you can click on it to conveniently launch the app from the Dock.

When you move the cursor tool over an icon in the Dock, it pops up a little label with the name of that app ❷. In addition, you can **ctr+click** on an app icon in the Dock for even more features.

➡ Attention

Ctr+click on the app icon on the Dock to open a menu with the following commands:

💀 Bottom Three

The commands on the bottom ❸ vary and depend on the status of the app:

- ▶ **Quit/Open**: If the app is not running, then the *Open* command lets you launch it. If the app is running, then the displayed command will be *Quit*.
- ▶ **Show/Show Recent**: If the app is already running, then the Show command will bring it to the front. If Logic is not running, then the command will be "Show Recent", which will switch the screen to Mission Control, showing the most recently opened Logic Projects as icons at the bottom of the screen ❹. These are the same Projects listed in Logic's *File ➤ Open Recent ➤* submenu. 
- ▶ **Show all Windows**: This is another OSX Mission Control command that I discuss on the next page.

💀 Options

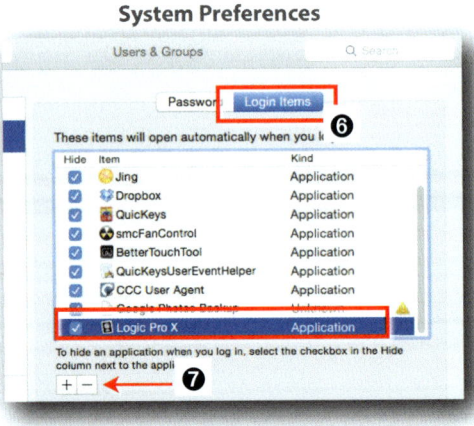

The Options ❺ command is a submenu with the following commands:

- ▶ **Keep in Dock/Remove from Dock**: If you want to have the Logic app visible in the Dock even after you quit it, choose the "*Keep in Dock*" command. At any time, when Logic is not running, use the "*Remove from Dock*" command to remove it from the Dock so it is only visible when launched.
- ▶ **Open at Login**: This command adds Logic to the list of Login Items ❻ in the *System Preferences ➤ Users & Groups* so it launches automatically when starting the computer. Remove that functionality by selecting it again to uncheck it, or in the System Preferences, *click* the minus button ❼.
- ▶ **Show in Finder**: This is the standard command that opens the Finder window where the application file is located.

App Specific

The section above the Options menu has commands that are specific to that app. In the case of Logic, there are two sections:

- **Open Recent ❶**: The section at the very top lists all the recently opened Logic Projects (Set the maximum number of displayed items in the *System Preferences ➤ General ➤ Recent Items*). These are the same items that are listed in Logic's *File ➤ Open Recent ➤* submenu ❷. That means, you can launch any of these Logic Projects directly from the Dock.

- **Open Window ❸**: This section is identical to the bottom section of Logic's Window Menu ❹. That means, you can open a specific window, bring it to the front directly from the Dock, even when another app is currently in the foreground.

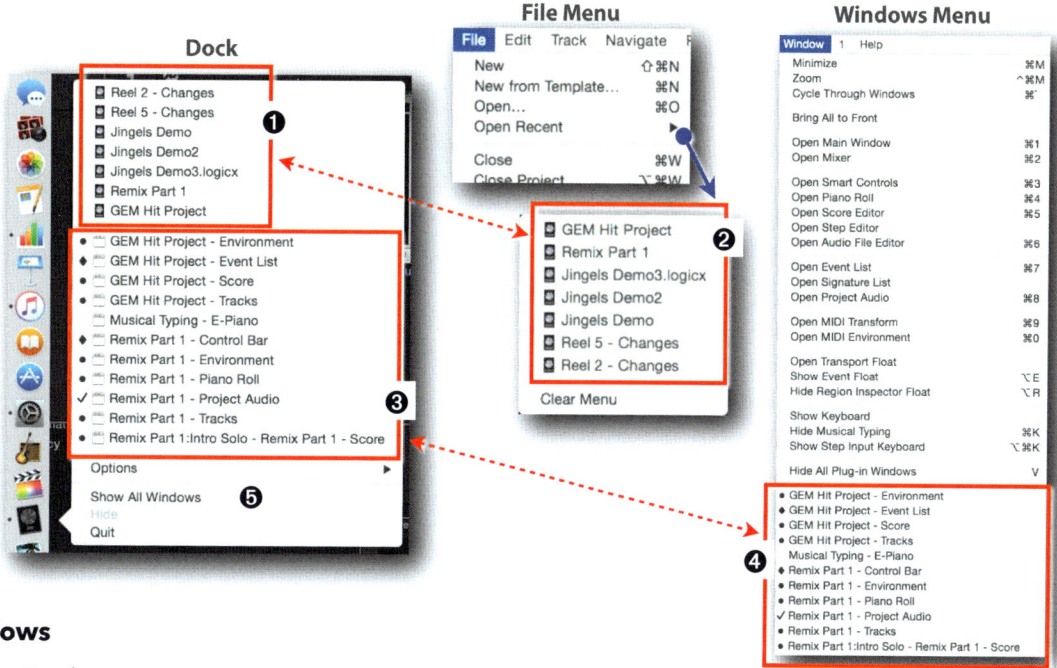

Show All Windows

This command in the Dock menu ❺ is an OSX Mission Control command. It has the same functionality as the "Application windows" ❻ command with its assigned Key Command in the *System Preferences ➤ Mission Control*. It switches the computer screen to the Mission Control view, shrinking all the Logic Windows so they can fit on the screen next to each other without overlapping ❼. This provides a quick overview of all the currently open windows in Logic and lets you choose a window (bringing to the foreground) by *clicking* on it, which will exit Mission Control view.

Please note that at the bottom of the Mission Control view, all the recently opened Logic Projects are listed ❽.

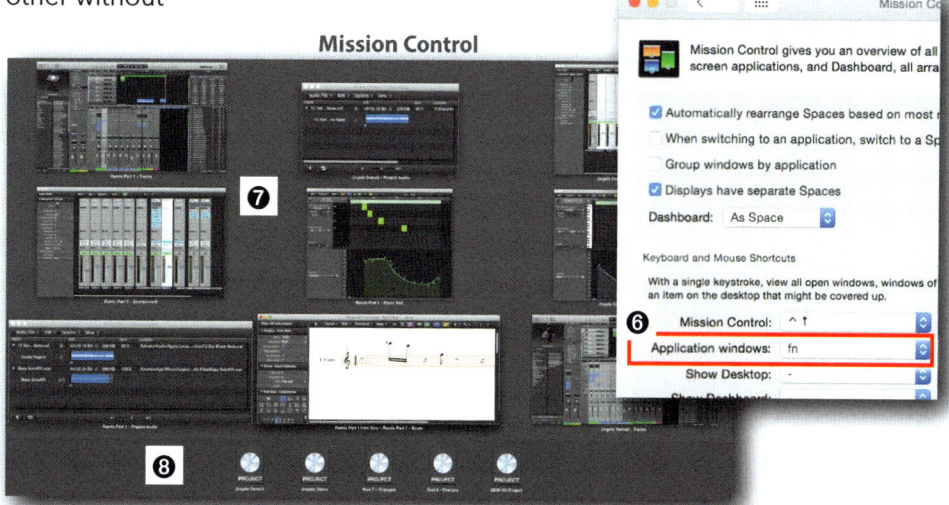

You can set the behaviors for the Dock in the *System Preferences ➤ Dock*. Set it to *"Automatically hide and show the Dock"* when you move the Cursor Tool over it. You can toggle that setting with the system Key Command **opt+cmd+D** to show the Dock.

Miscellaneous

How to Import/Export the Custom Configuration in the Plug-in Manager

➡ Review

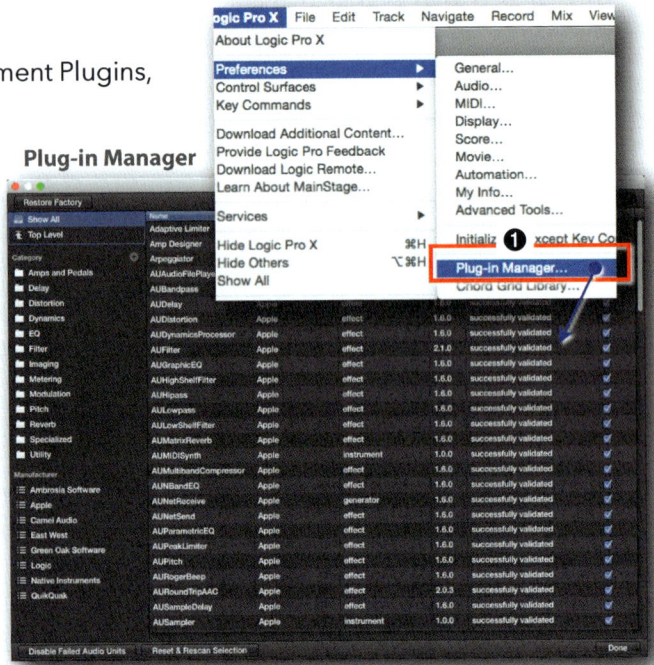

Logic has three types of Plugin Menus: Software Instrument Plugins, Audio FX Plugins, and MIDI FX Plugins. You open them by clicking on the Plugin Buttons on the Channel Strip. The menus list all the available (installed) Plugins in a default order.

LPX v10.1 introduced a new feature called the "Plug-in Manager", which lets you customize the menus and organize them differently, even creating your own subfolders.

You open the Plug-in Manager with any of the two commands:

- Main Menu *Logic Pro X ➤ Preferences ➤ Plug-In Manager...* ❶
- Key Command (*Plug-in Manager...*)
  unassigned

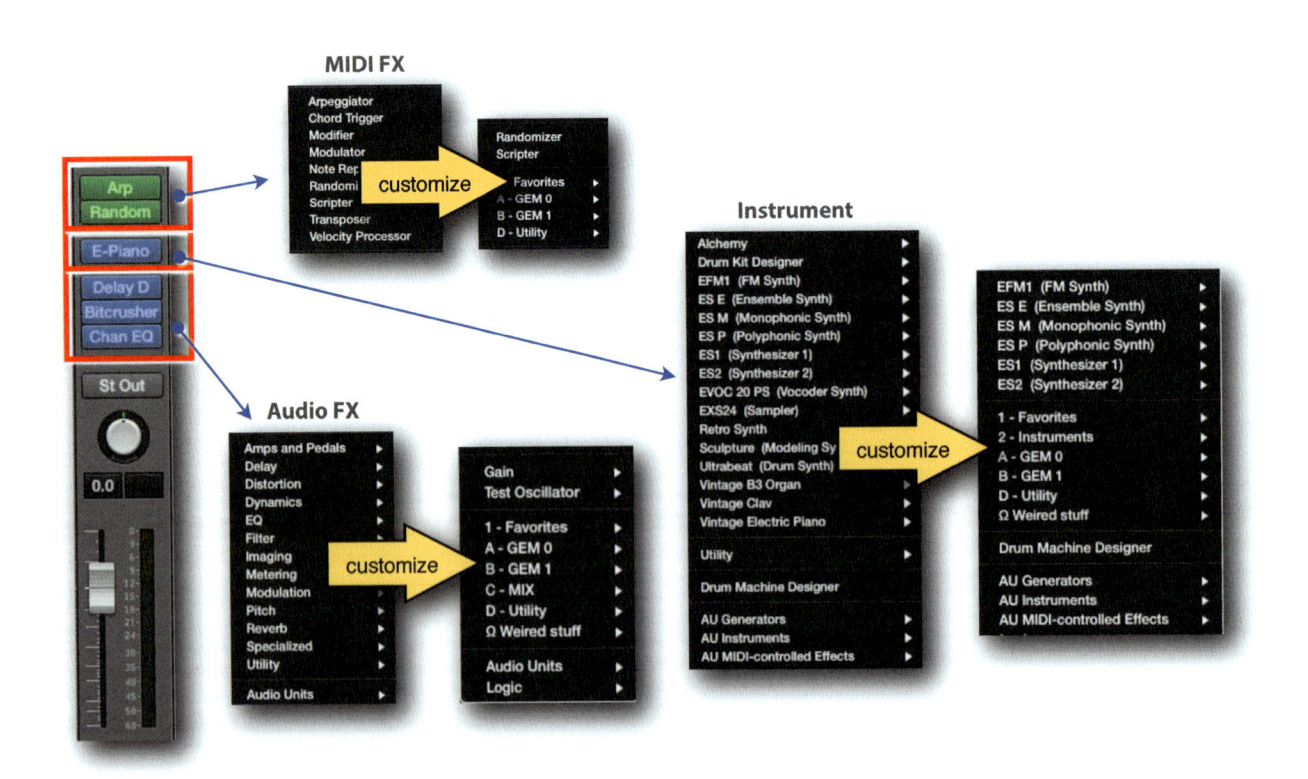

40   2 - Hidden Features

➡ **Problem**

The limitation is that you only have one configuration, the one you are currently configuring in that window. The only other option is to reset the window to the default configuration (*clicking* on the "Restore Factory" Button in the upper left corner of the Plug-in Manager). There is currently no export or import feature in Logic v10.2 that lets you manage different configurations similar to the Key Command Sets. But where there's a will, there's a way.

➡ **Solution**

Here is how you create and manage individual Plug-in Manager Configuration Sets:

The Underlying Concept

Whenever you make a change in the Plug-in Manager Window, Logic stores those changes to various files in a specific folder that is visible in the Finder. Whenever you launch Logic, it reads those files to recreate your personal configuration for the Plugin Menus.

Logic doesn't store the Plugin configuration as one single settings file, it creates a whole group of files. They are stored inside the Tags folder ❶, which is stored inside the Databases folder, which is stored in the important Audio Music Apps folder where Logic keeps all its various settings files.

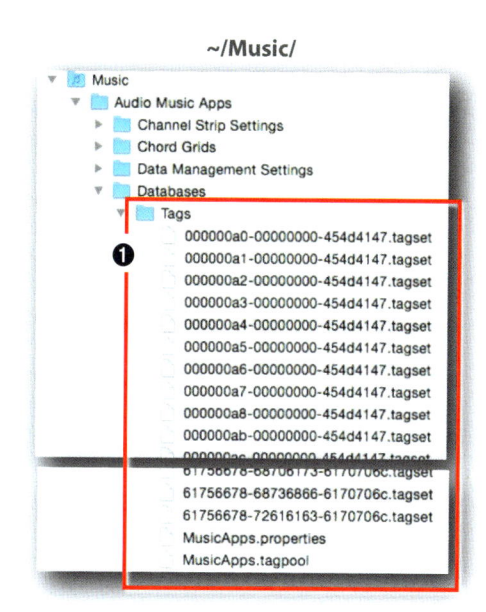

~/Music/Audio Music Apps/Databases/Tags/

Procedure

▸ **Import/Export Sets**: To import or export a specific Plug-in Manager Configuration Set, you just swap the Tags folder in the Finder. Make sure that Logic is not launched during this operation.

- *Export*: Once you have configured the Plug-in Manager, you just quit Logic and copy the Tags folder in the Finder to a new location. You can even create different configurations and store those different Tags folders.
- *Import*: To import a different Plug-in Manager Configuration Set, quit Logic, delete the current Tags folder, and move one of the Tags folder that you have copied before to a different location back into the Databases location. Launch Logic and it's there.

▸ **Exchange Sets**: You can exchange those Tags folders with other computers in your studio or with other users (assuming they have the same collection of Plugins).

▸ **Reset**: If you completely delete the Tags folder, launch Logic, and open the Plug-in Manager, you will see the default configuration. This is the same effect as *clicking* on the *Restore Factory Button* ❷ in the upper left corner of the Plug-in Manager. Once you make your first changes in that window, Logic creates a new Tags folder with its corresponding files.

▸ **XML files**: The files in the Tags folder are XML files, so you can open them in a text editor to understand how Logic is doing its magic.

Tempo Sets Store Individual Synchronization Settings

➡ **Review**

No matter if you only have one constant Tempo throughout your Project or have created an elaborate Tempo Curve with Tempo changes, accelerandi, etc., all that information is stored in the Project's Tempo Track. However, Logic has not just one but nine independent Tempo Tracks, the so-called *Tempo Sets*. This is a great feature that lets you experiment with different tempo settings by switching back and forth between Tempo Sets.

Create a new Tempo Set from the Tempo Set popup menu (available from the Tempo List ❶ or the Global Track ❷). Now, adjust the Tempos in that Tempo Set and conveniently switch between the Sets by selecting them from the Tempo Set menu.

➡ **Attention**

The Tempo Sets store one setting in addition to the Tempo Information, and that is the "*Bar Position X plays at SMPTE Y*" that is set in the *Project Settings* ➤ *Synchronization* ➤ *General* ❸. This setting is mainly used when scoring to picture in order to line up a specific Bar Position to a specific SMPTE Position. I cover all the information about that tricky subject in the Synchronization chapter of my book "Logic Pro X - The Details".

For example, if you need to swap different movie files in your Project that require different sync settings, then you can use the Tempo Sets to switch between them without changing the Sync Setting every time.

Here is an example with three different Tempo Sets ❹:

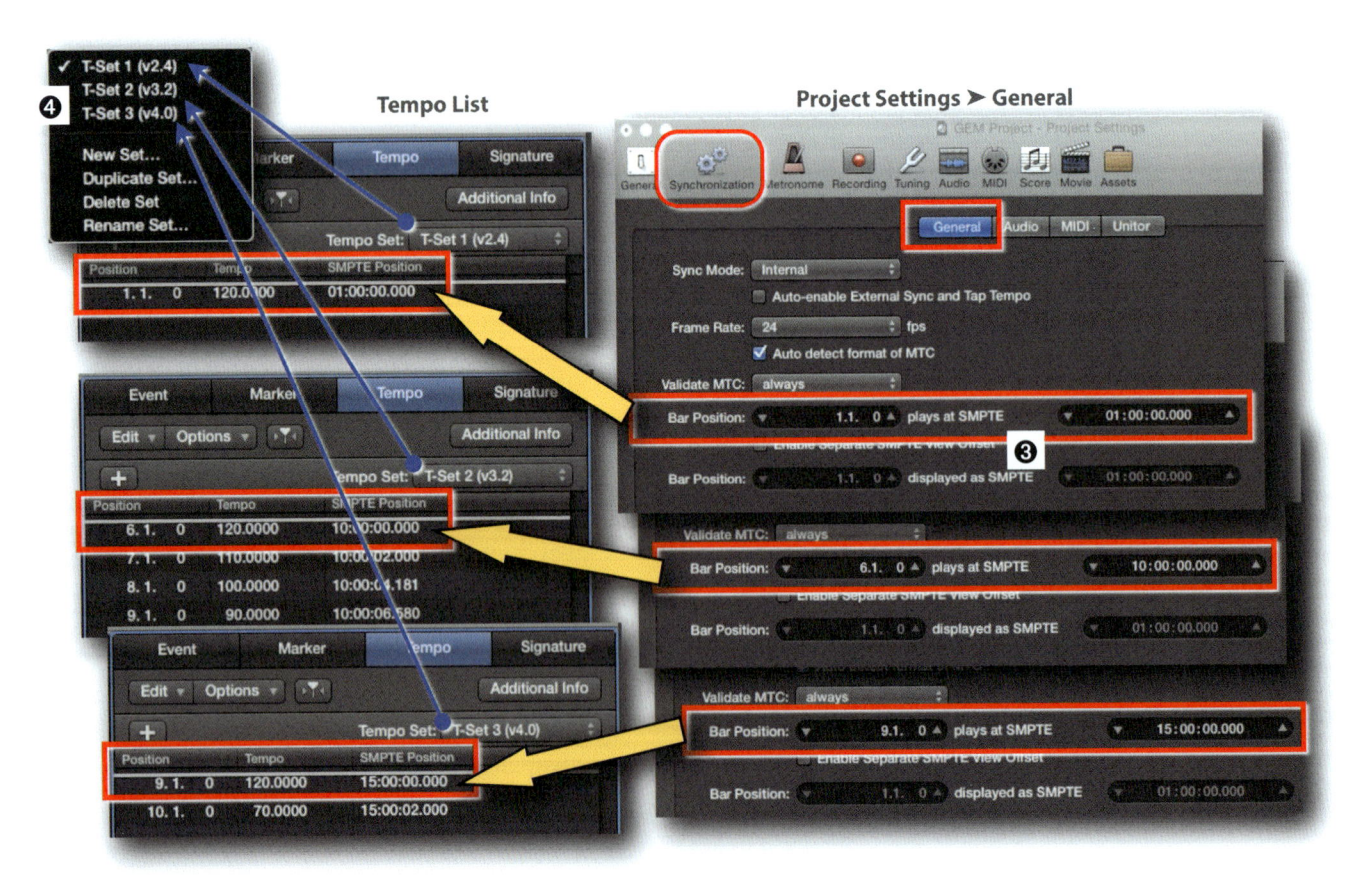

42   2 - Hidden Features

3 - Special Click Actions

Tracks Window

Close Window Panes by Double-Clicking on a Header or Divider Line

➡ **Review**

Logic's Main Window follows the concept of a single window work environment. You can stay in one window and most of the other needed windows can be shown/hidden in a section of the Main Window, as so-called Window Panes.

In Logic, the Tracks Window ❶ is the center and all other Window Panes can be shown/hidden to the left, right, at the bottom, and at the top as needed. The View Menu ❷ contains all the commands to toggle those Window Panes.

➡ **Attention**

Sometimes you don't want to take your hands off the mouse or trackpad, or your cursor is already near the Window Pane anyways. In that case, there are some hidden click actions to close and even open various Window Panes:

- **Double-click** on the Header of a Window Pane to close it. For example, the Library Window Header ❸.
- If the Window Pane has multiple Tabs in the Header, then you can **double-click** on the active (blue) tab to close the Window Pane ❹.
- Moving the Cursor Tool over a Divider Line changes it to one of the Resize Tools. **Double-click** on those vertical or horizontal Divider Lines ❺ between the Window Pane and its adjacent window to close that Window Pane.
- You can even **double-click** on the outer edge of the Main Window (when a Window Pane is hidden) to open that Window Pane. However, this functionality doesn't seem to work reliably.

3 - Special Click Actions

Track Icons Click Functionality

➡ *Review*

The Track Icons have more functions than just providing a graphical indication of what's on that Track. There are quite a few useful click actions you should know about.

➡ *Attention*

Please note that Track Icons can actually be displayed in five different places:

💀 **Track Header**

▸ *Click*: This will select the Track ❶, or, in the case of a Track Stack, toggles the Stack open/close (same as clicking on the disclosure triangle).

▸ *Double-click*: This click action depends on three conditions:
  - **Library Window ❷**: If no Patch is loaded on that Track, then the Library Window will open/close.
  - **Smart Controls ❸**: If a Patch is loaded on that Track, then the Smart Controls window pane at the bottom of Logic's Main Window will open/close.
  - **Drum Machine Designer Window** (DMD) ❹: If the Track is a Main Track or Subtrack of the DMD, then the DMD Window will open/close.

▸ *Cmd-click*: This will open the Plugin Window. Which one, depends on the Track Type:
  - **Instrument Plugin ❺**: It will open the Instrument Plugin.
  - **First FX Plugin ❻ or Channel EQ ❼**: It will open the first Audio FX Plugin, or the Channel EQ Plugin if it is loaded (in any slot).

▸ *Ctr+click*: This is the standard action to open the Track Icon Popover Window ❽.

💀 **Channel Strip**

▸ **Drum Machine Designer ❹**: The Track Icons only respond to one click action. If the Channel Strip belongs to a DMD (Main Track or Subtrack), then a *double-click* opens the DMD Window.

💀 **Library Window**

▸ **Drum Machine Designer ❹**: The Track Icon only responds to a click action if the Track belongs to a DMD (Main Track or Subtrack). A *double-click* opens the DMD Window.

💀 **Track Inspector (Tracks Window)**

▸ **Track Icon Popover ❽**: Any *click* action will open the Track Icon Popover Window.

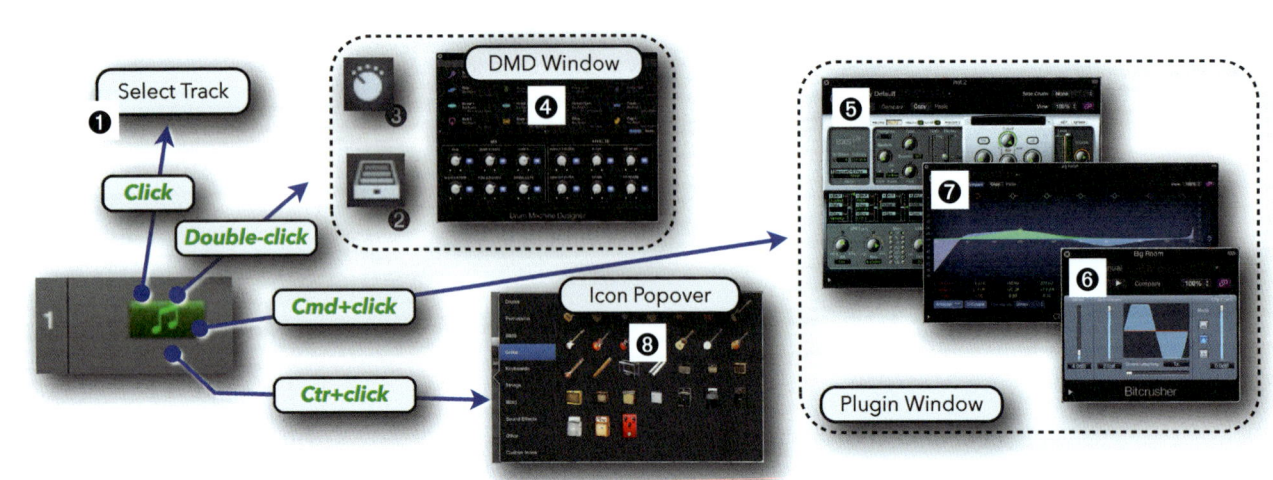

💀 **Instrument Inspector (Environment)**

▸ **Track Icon Popover ❽**: Any *click* action will open the Track Icon Popover Window.

44 3 - Special Click Actions

Create MIDI Region on an Audio Track

➡ Review

In Logic Pro 9 you could use the Pencil Tool ✏ to create MIDI Regions on the Track Lane not only for Software Instrument Tracks, but also for Audio Tracks. Unfortunately, in LPX that doesn't works anymore on Audio Tracks.

➡ Attention

Now in LPX when you *click* with the Pencil Tool ✏ on the Track Header of an Audio Track, it will open the Open File Dialog to select an Audio File to import and place its corresponding Audio Region at that clicked position. To create a MIDI Region on an Audio Track, you have to *sh+click* with the Pencil Tool.

These are the two commands now:

- *Click* with Pencil Tool on the Track Lane of an Audio Track to create an Audio Region (import a new Audio File).
- *Sh+click* with Pencil Tool on the Track Lane of an Audio Track to create a MIDI Region.

Please note that LPX doesn't allow you to create any Region on an Output Track (Track assigned to an Output Channel Strip) or Master Track (Track assigned to the Master Channel Strip).

Select/Deselect All Events on a Global Track

➡ Review

There are many actions to select Events, Control Points, or other objects, but there are special ones for the Global Tracks.

➡ Attention

Select All: *Click* on the Header of any Global Track (except the Movie Track) to select all the events on that Track.

Toggle Selection: *Sh+click* on the Header of any Track (except the Movie Track) to toggle the current selection. Selected objects become unselected, and unselected objects become selected.

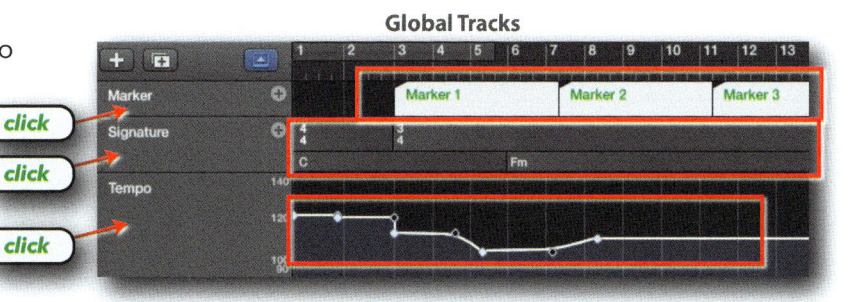

3 - Special Click Actions

Option+Click on a Parameter to Reset it to Default Value

➡ **Review**

Logic provides a convenient way to reset an onscreen control (Fader, Slider, Knob) to its default value.
For example:
- *Opt+click* on a Volume Fader to set it to Unity Gain, 0dB
- *Opt+click* on a Pan Knob to set it to the center position
- *Opt+click* on an Aux Send Knob to set it to 0dB
- *Opt+click* on any onscreen control in a Plugin Window or Smart Controls Window

This "option key" click action also works for most of the numeric values of Parameters and not only in the Mixer Window.

➡ **Attention**

Inspector

You can *opt+click* on almost any parameter in the Inspector ❶ to reset it to its default value ❷. Please note that there is a checkbox in the **Preferences ➤ Display ➤ General ➤ "Show default values"** ❸. Deselect it to only show values if they are not default values ❹. I prefer this option because it is easier to spot the important settings, the ones that are not default.

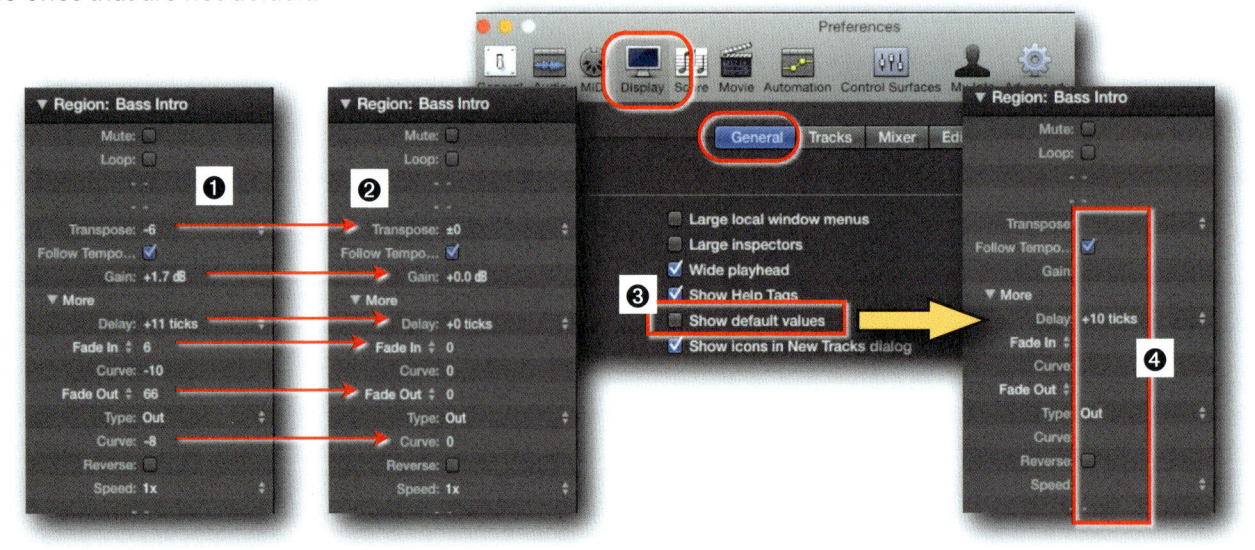

Plugins and other windows

The *opt+click* action also works on almost any other window that provides numeric entries for parameter values, like parameters on Plugin Windows ❺.

46   3 - Special Click Actions

Choose a Flex Mode for Multiple or All Tracks

➡ *Review*

Here is a summary of the basic setup rules when choosing a Flex Mode:
- ▸ You can choose from seven different Flex Modes ❶.
- ▸ You can only choose one Flex Mode for a Track at a time and that Flex Mode applies to all Regions on that Track.
- ▸ You can choose a Flex Mode for a Track from three places:
  - In the Track Inspector ❷.
  - On the Track Header ❸ (when Flex Mode is made visible with the Show/Hide Flex Button ❹ 🔲).
  - In the Audio Track Editor ❺ (when Flex Mode is made visible with the Show/Hide Flex Button ❻ 🔲).
- ▸ You can temporarily enable/disable Flex for an entire Track with the "Enable Flex Button" ❼ 🔲, or enable/disable Flex for individual Regions with the Flex checkbox ❽ in the Region Inspector.

In addition, there are a few more hidden actions for choosing a Flex Mode.

➡ *Attention*

There are three actions for setting the Flex Mode for one or multiple Tracks:

🎱 **Choose a Flex Mode for one Track**

To set a single Track to a specific Flex Mode, choose from any of the three places I just showed (Track Inspector ❷, Track Header ❸, Audio Track Editor ❺).

🎱 **Choose a Flex Mode for all selected Tracks**

If you want to set a specific Flex Mode to multiple Tracks, then you can do that with one action. Select all the Tracks in the Tracks Window and choose the Flex Mode from the Track Header ❸ on one of the selected Tracks. All the selected Tracks will be set to that Flex Mode.

🎱 **Choose a Flex Mode for all Tracks in your Project**

Click on the Flex Mode Menu of the Track Header ❸ on any of your Tracks and then *sh+click* on a Flex Mode on that Menu ❾ when making the selection. All Tracks in your Project will then be set to that specific Flex Mode.

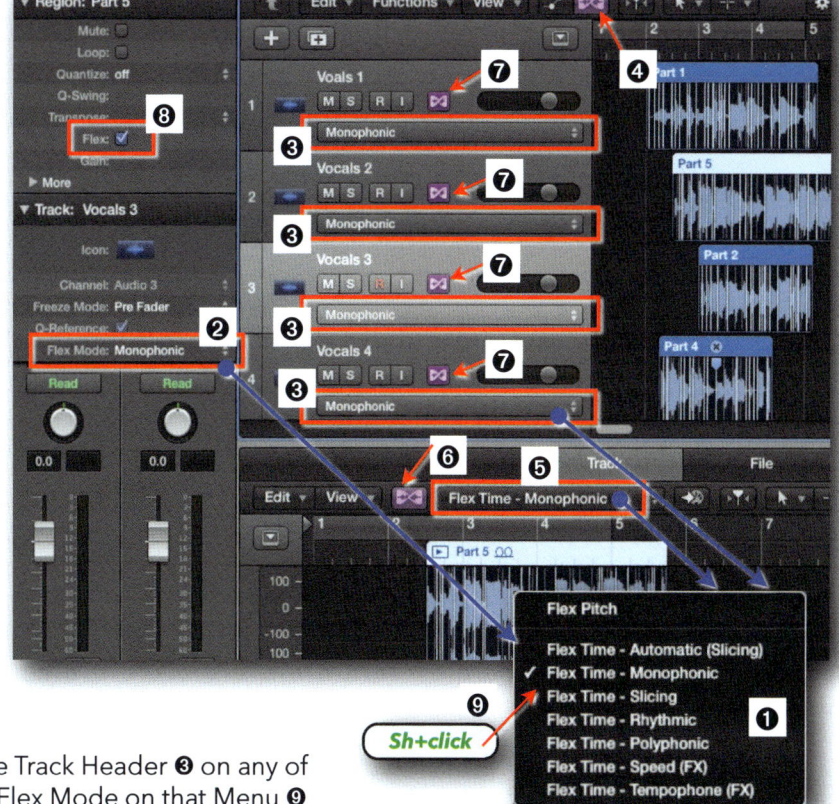

3 - Special Click Actions 47

Toggle Configuration Windows with Their Key Command

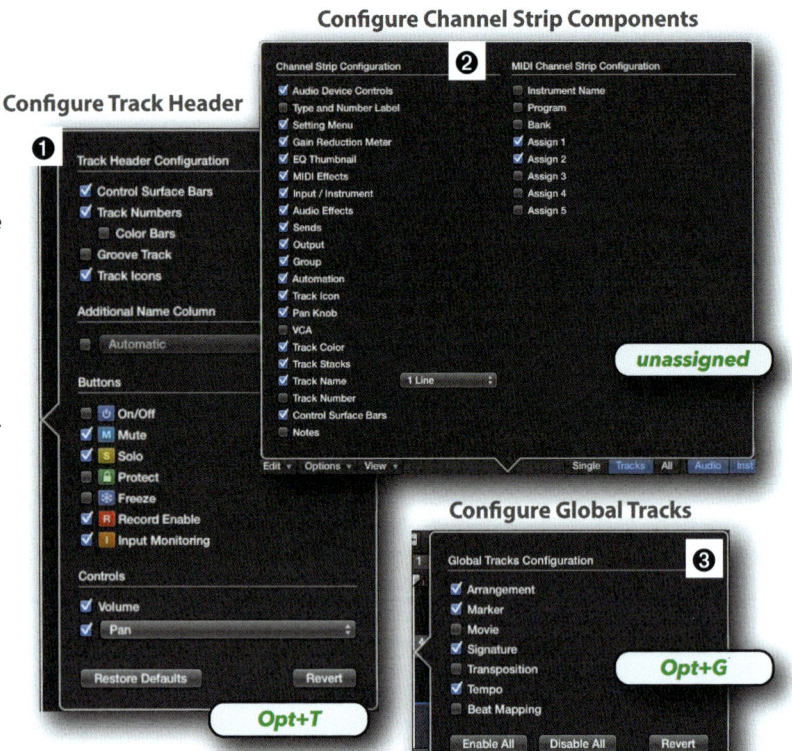

➡ **Review**

Logic uses a special type of window, a so-called Popover, mainly for configuration windows. I discuss their differences compared to Sheets (another type of window) a little later. Here are three of those Popover windows that have something in common:

➡ **Attention**

There is a special configuration window for the Track Header and the Channel Strip that lets you setup which components are visible. Another configuration window for the Global Tracks lets you setup which Global Tracks are displayed.

All three windows have a dedicated Key Command that lets you open the window. However, unlike other windows, those Key Commands also let you close the window, making them "toggle" commands. I wish that functionality would be implemented in all Key Commands that open windows.

- ▶ **Configure Track Header** ❶: Key Command *opt+T*
- ▶ **Configure Channel Strip Components** ❷: Key Command *"unassigned"*
- ▶ **Configure Global Tracks** ❸: Key Command *opt+G*

Long Click on Primary Ruler Enables Cycle Mode

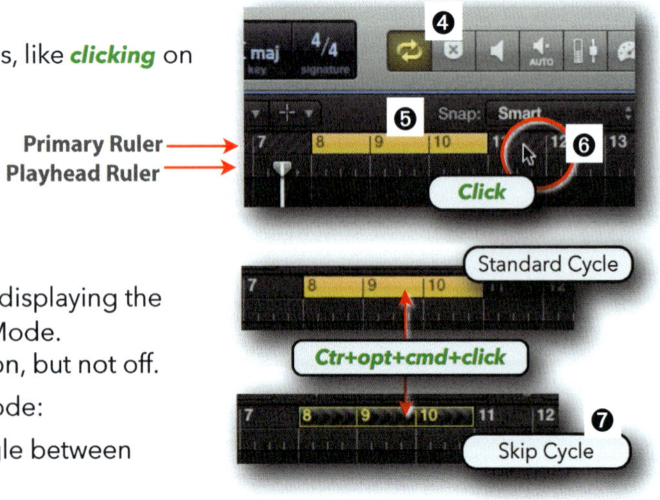

➡ **Review**

You can toggle the Cycle Mode with various commands, like *clicking* on the Cycle Mode Button ❹, use the Key Command *C*, or *clicking* on the Cycle Range ❺ itself. However, there is one other action.

➡ **Attention**

A *long-click* anywhere on the Primary Ruler ❻, the area displaying the time units and the Cycle Range, will enable the Cycle Mode. Unfortunately, this only works for turning Cycle Mode on, but not off.

Here are two more useful click actions for the Cycle Mode:

- 💡 *Ctr+opt+cmd+click* on the Cycle Range to toggle between Standard Cycle and Skip Cycle ❼.
- 💡 *Sh+click* on the Primary Ruler to extend the Cycle Range to the click position on the left or right.

48   3 - Special Click Actions

Change Priority for Coloring Regions/Tracks

➡ Review

You can color Regions or Tracks by selecting them ❶ and then *click* a color on the Color Palette Window ❷ (*opt+C*). But there is a specific priority to be aware of.

➡ Attention

Please note that in the Tracks Window you can have a Track selected and no Regions, but you can never have Regions selected and no Track. At least one Track is always selected.

- ▶ *Click* on a Color: The selected Track(s) is only colored if no Regions are selected. If you have any Regions selected ❶, then they have priority and the selected color will change the selected Region ❸ and not the selected Track(s).

- ▶ *Cmd+click* on a Color: This command overwrites any Region priority. Only the selected Track(s) ❹ will change color, no matter if there are Regions selected ❺ or not.

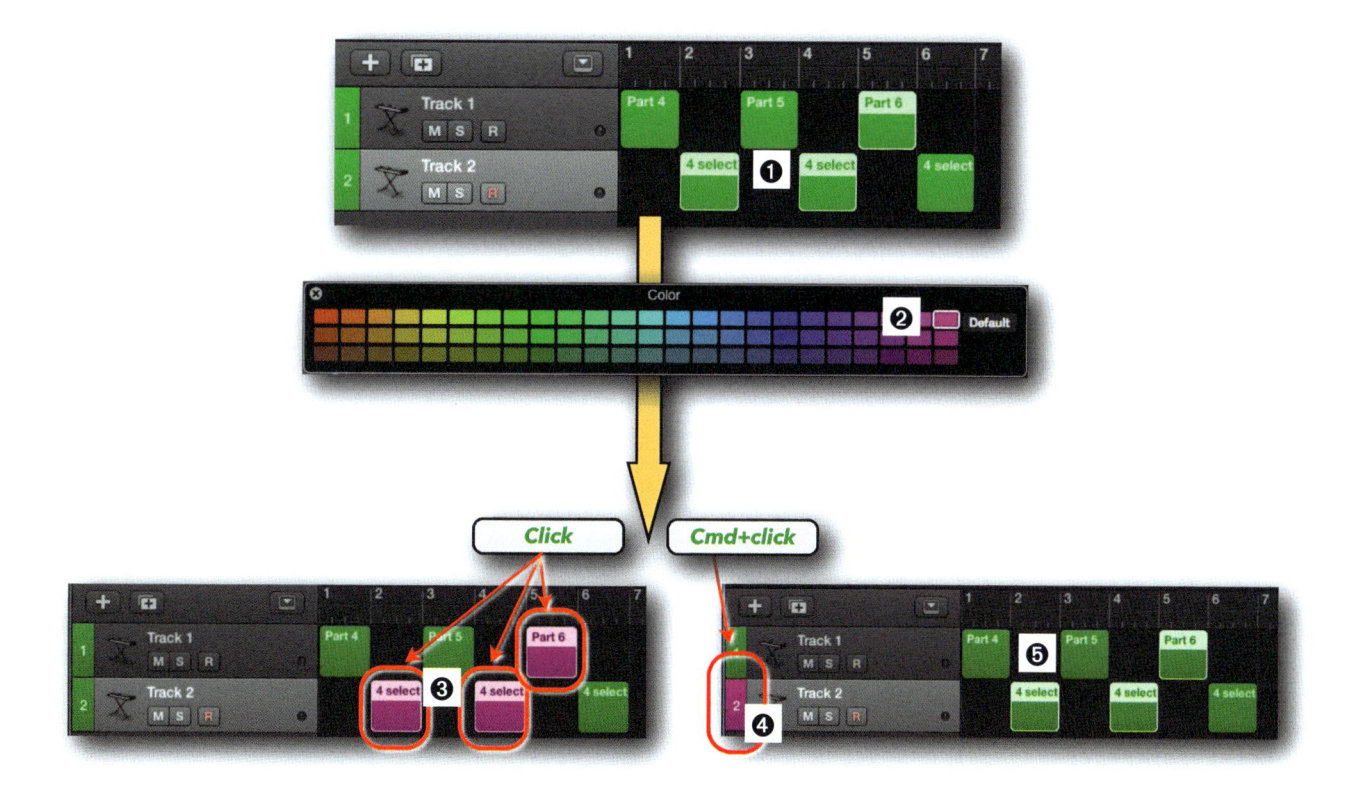

3 - Special Click Actions

Two Different Solo Tools

➡ **Review**

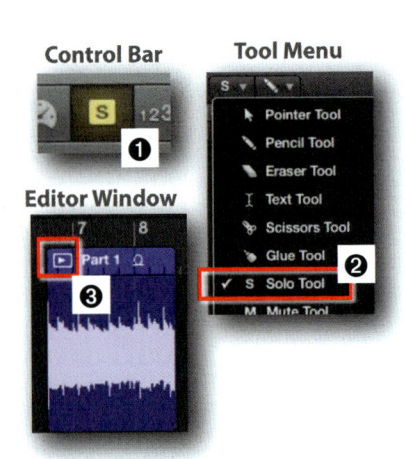

Logic has two types of Solo Modes:
- **Channel Strip Solo** ("transmission"): This solo mode affects the transmission of an audio signal. Selecting the Solo Button on a Channel Strip or Track Header will solo that Channel Strip and mutes any other Channel Strip that is not soloed.
- **Region Solo** ("source"): This solo mode affects the source of the signal, the Regions. All the Channel Strips are "open", but the solo mode lets only the soloed Regions play. Other non-soloed Regions are temporarily muted (grayed out). You can select the Region Solo by toggling the Solo Mode Button ❶ on the Control Bar or use the Key Command (*Solo Mode*) *ctr+S*. The various Editor Windows display a special Solo Play Button ❸ on the Region Header that can also be used to play back only that Region. In addition, you can change the Pointer Tool to the Solo Tool by selecting it from the Tool Menu ❷.

However, there is special attention needed when using the Solo Tool.

➡ **Attention**

There are not one, but two Solo Tools with slightly different functionalities:

- *Click-hold* with the Solo Tool on a Region ❹: 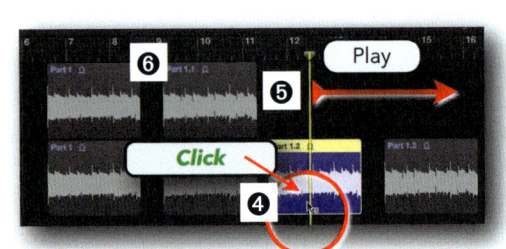
    - The Playhead starts at the clicked position ❺ and plays back that Region. It keeps on playing until you release the mouse.
    - The rules for what Regions are soloed are a bit complex (confusing) with many different conditions:
        - If no Region was selected prior, then the Region you click on with the Solo Tool will be selected during playback and all other Regions will appear darkened (muted) ❻.
        - If multiple Regions are selected prior and you click on one of the selected Regions, then the Region you click on and all the other selected Regions are soloed during Playback.
        - If multiple Regions are selected prior but you click on an unselected Region, then only the clicked-on Region will be soloed and all other Regions will be darkened (muted). Please note that after you release the mouse, only the clicked-on Region stays selected.
        - When you just click on Region (not click-hold), then other Regions are muted. This seems to follow some strange rules that I think are not worth remembering (it's too much). Just click the Solo Mode Button to reset all the soloed Regions.

- *Opt+click-hold* with the Solo Tool on a Region ❼: 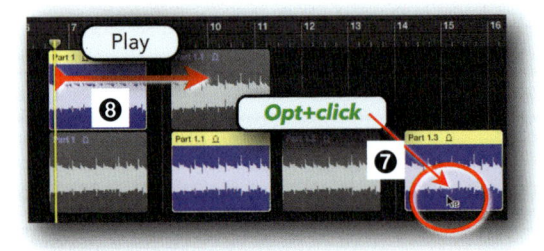
    - The Playhead starts to play from the beginning of the clicked Region instead of the clicked position.
    - The rules for what Regions are soloed are the same for both Solo Tools with one exception:
        - The playback starts at the beginning of the first selected Region ❽, no mater which selected Region you click on.

50   3 - Special Click Actions

Click Zone Rules for Cursor Tool in the Track Lane

➡ **Review**

The Tool Menu in the Tracks Window provides 14 Cursor Tools to choose from when editing Regions in the Tracks Window. However, the actual Tool might change due to Click Zones (specific areas that act as hot spots), settings, and modifier keys. This makes it almost impossible to predict what Tool is displayed and when.

➡ **Attention**

To better show all the rules and exceptions for the various Tools, I organize them into four groups based on a hierarchy of rules:

💀 **1 - Overwrites**

There are two key combinations that overwrite any other rules regarding the Cursor Tool:
- ▶ **Zoom Overwrite**: Holding down the *ctr+opt* keys always switches to the Zoom Tool when hovering anywhere over a Region. When hovering anywhere on the Workspace outside a Region, it requires holding down only the *opt* key.
- ▶ **Fade Overwrite**: Holding down the *sh+ctr* keys always switches to the Fade Tool when hovering over the left or right border of an Audio Region.

💀 **2 - Tools without Click Zones**

The following Tools don't have any Click Zones or other conditions. That means, no matter where you move the cursor on the Region, the Tool always stays the same. It will only change with the two overwrite key combinations for Zoom and Fade that I just mentioned.
- ▶ **Erase**
- ▶ **Text**
- ▶ **Glue**
- ▶ **Mute**
- ▶ **Zoom**
- ▶ **Automation Select Tool**
- ▶ **Automation Curve Tool**
- ▶ **Marquee**

💀 **3 - Tools without Click Zones, but with variations**

The following Tools also don't have any Click Zones. However, they have "variations" for multiple functionalities:
- ▶ **Scissors**: Holding down the *option* key switches the standard Scissors Tool to the Scissors Tool with a plus symbol. Now instead of making one split, a click on the Region splits the Region into multiple, equal parts based on the distance between the Region start and the click position.
- ▶ **Solo**: I explained that functionality with the two Solo Tools in the previous section.
- ▶ **Fade**: The Fade Tool displays the Fade Length (hovering over the beginning or end of the Fade) or the Fade Curve (hovering between the beginning and end of the shaded Fade area).

💀 **4 - Tools with Click Zones**

3 - Special Click Actions

These are the four Tools that need the most attention. They can change based on three factors:
- **Click Zones**: There are up to three Click Zones on the left and right border of a Region (top, middle, bottom). I indicate them in these diagrams with red lines.
- **Preferences**: The *Preferences ➤ General ➤ Editing* has two checkboxes ❶ that can affect the Click Zones.
- **Modifier Key**: Whenever the Click Zone changes the Tool to the Resize Tool, you can hold down the *option* key to change to the Compress/Expand Tool.

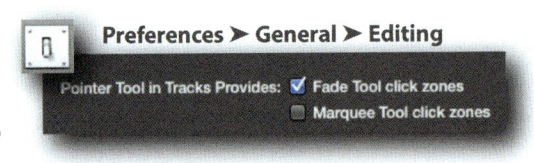

▶ **Pointer**:
The Pointer Tool is the most "flexible", or confusing, depending upon how you look at it.
- The Click Zones act differently depending on the Preferences setting ❷.
- The Fade Tool, of course, applies only to Audio Regions, MIDI Regions ignore it (left border) or default to the Loop Tool ❸ (right border).
- The Preference for the Marquee Click Zone ❶ affects the lower half of the Region area ❹, not its borders.

▶ **Pencil**:
The Click Zones for the Pencil Tool are much simpler. It only switches to the Resize Tools and the Loop Tool ❺ on the upper right border of the Region.

▶ **Solo**:
The Click Zones for the Solo Tools don't make much sense. They switch to the Resize Tool on the right border, but not the left ❻. Strangely enough, the Fade Preference ❼ switches the middle section of the right border to the Loop Tool ❽ (for Audio Regions and MIDI Regions).

▶ **Flex**:
The Click Zones for the Flex Tool are more consistent. The Resize Tool is available for the left and right border. The upper right area of the border switches to the Compress/Expand Tool ❾ for Audio Regions and to the Loop Tool ❿ for MIDI Regions.

Please keep in mind that you have three separate Tool Menus. You switch those with the *cmd* key or the *ctr* key. Try to apply these modifier keys to the rules I showed so far, and things will get really interesting.

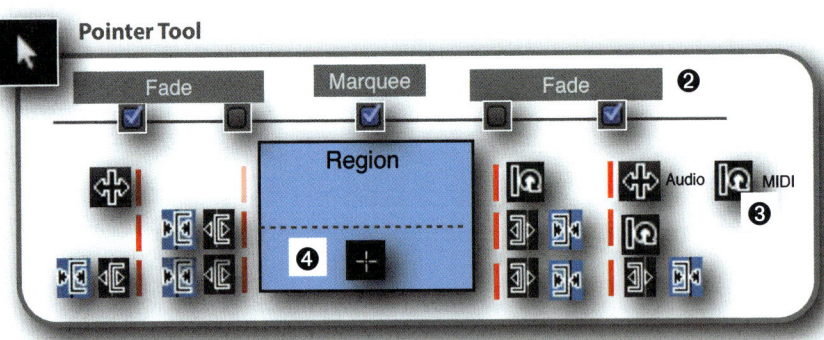

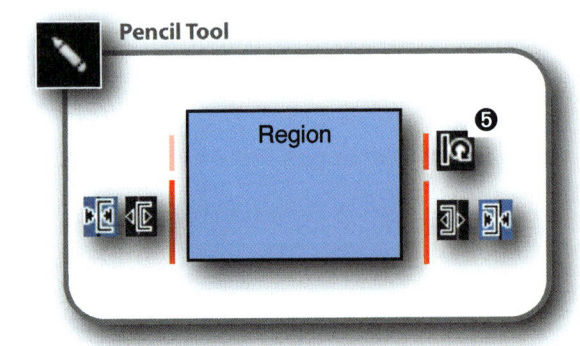

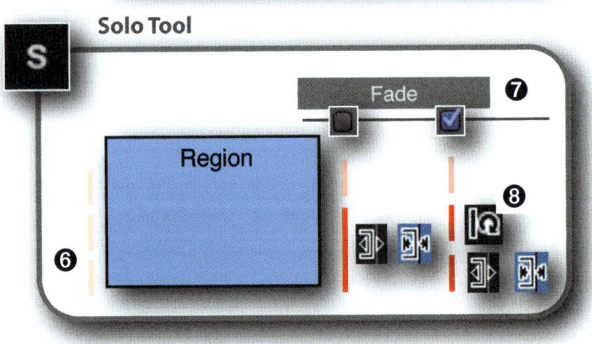

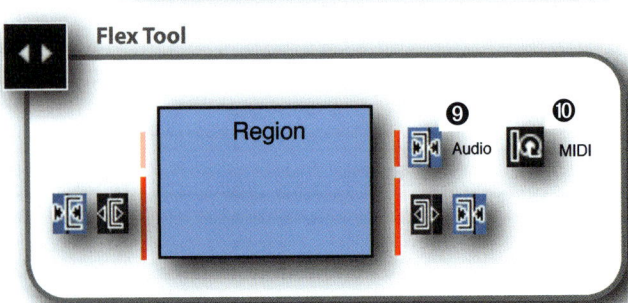

Piano Roll

Three "Priority" Tools in the Piano Roll

➡ Review

The Piano Roll Editor provides its own set of Tools in the Tool Menu ❶, and similar to the Tracks Window, there are rules and conditions that can overwrite the selected Tool, displaying a different Tool. Remember that you also have three Tool Menus available in the Editor Windows (standard-click Tool, command-click Tool, control-click Tool).

Tool Menu (Piano Roll)
- Pointer Tool ❶
- Pencil Tool
- Eraser Tool
- Finger Tool
- Scissors Tool
- Glue Tool
- Mute Tool
- Quantize Tool
- Velocity Tool
- Zoom Tool
- Automation Select Tool
- Automation Curve Tool
- Brush Tool

➡ Attention

There are three Tools that have priority in the Piano Roll and overwrite the currently selected Tool:

● Resize Tool

The left ❷ and right ❸ edge of a Note Event functions as an active Click Zone. Move the Cursor Tool over there and it changes to the Resize Tool to quickly resize the Note Event without switching Tools.

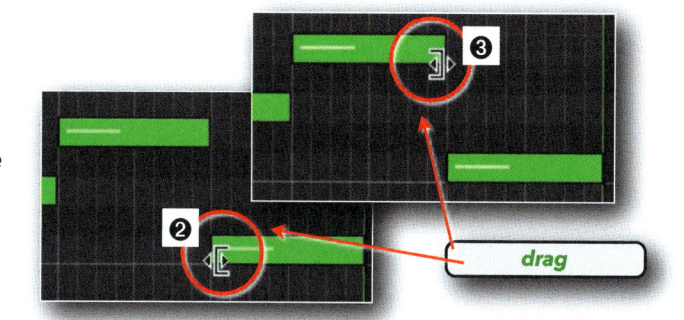

● Zoom Tool `Ctr+opt`

Holding down the **ctr+opt** keys in the Piano Roll Editor (in the Notes Area or the MIDI Draw Area) will switch the current Cursor Tool to the Zoom Tool.

- **Drag** a selection to zoom in ❹.
- **Click** on the background to zoom out (one zoom level at a time).

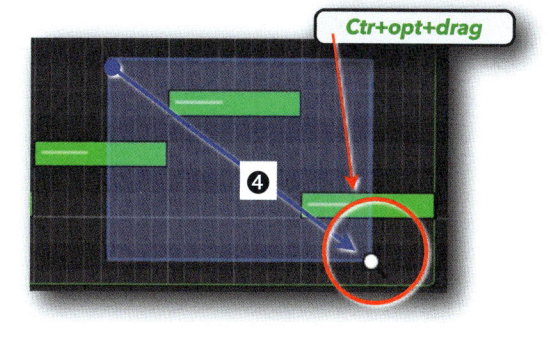

● Velocity Tool `Ctr+cmd`

Holding down the **ctr+cmd** keys when hovering over a Note Event will switch the current Cursor Tool to the Velocity Tool.

- **Drag** up and down to increase or decrease the Velocity value.
- The value of the Velocity Slider ❺, in the Local Inspector, changes accordingly while dragging up/down.
- You can select multiple Note Events and **ctr+cmd+drag** one of the Note Events to change the Velocity of all Note Events proportionally.

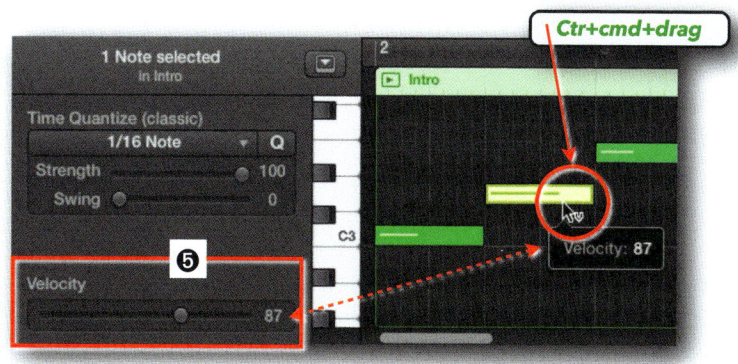

3 - Special Click Actions

Overwrite Min and Max Velocity Value of a Group of Notes

➡ **Review**

There are many procedures on how to change the velocity values of a group of MIDI Notes. Each one has a slightly different behavior, which makes it hard to memorize the different steps.

➡ **Attention**

To better compare the different procedures and behaviors when changing velocity values of a group of selected MIDI Notes ❶, I compare three aspects:

- ▶ **Operation**: This describes the basic procedure on how to change the values.
- ▶ **Relation between Values**: This describes what happens to the relationship between the different velocity values of those selected Notes when changing the values.
- ▶ **Limits when moving**: This describe what happens when a value reaches its limit, either the maximum value (127) ❷ or the minimum value (1) ❸. There are two scenarios you have to be aware of:
  - Group Limit: What I mean by that is you cannot move the entire group any further in one direction if any velocity value of one note in that group reaches its minimum ❹ or maximum value ❺.
  - Individual Limits: What I mean by that is if the velocity value of any note in the group of selected notes reaches the minimum ❸ or maximum ❷ value when dragging, the other values continue until each individual value reaches their limit ❻. This, by the way, is a procedure that lets you set all velocity values to the same value. Once they all have a value of 127 or 1, you can move them up or down as the same value.

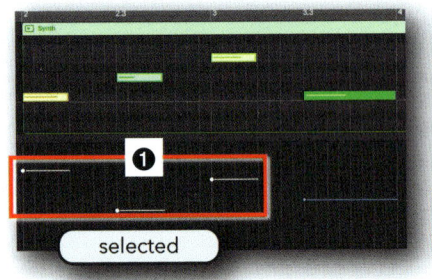

Original Selection

Group Limit

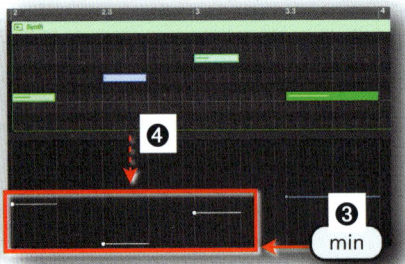

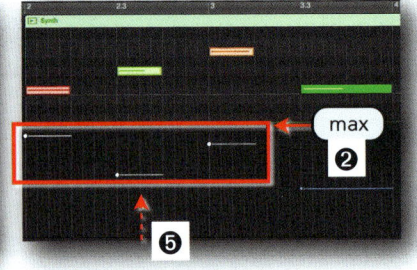

Individual Limit

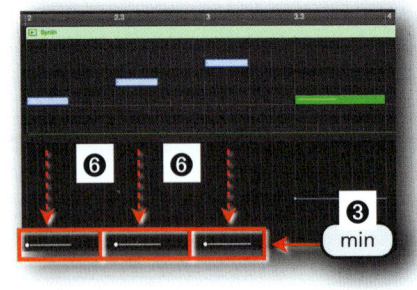

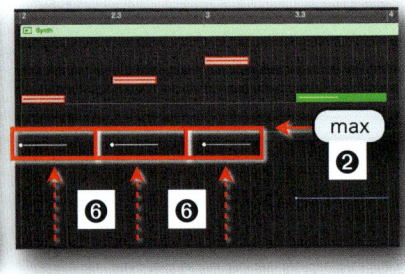

Now let's look at the different areas in the Piano Roll where you can change the velocity values. The procedures are similar in the Score Editor.

- 🟡 **MIDI Notes Area** 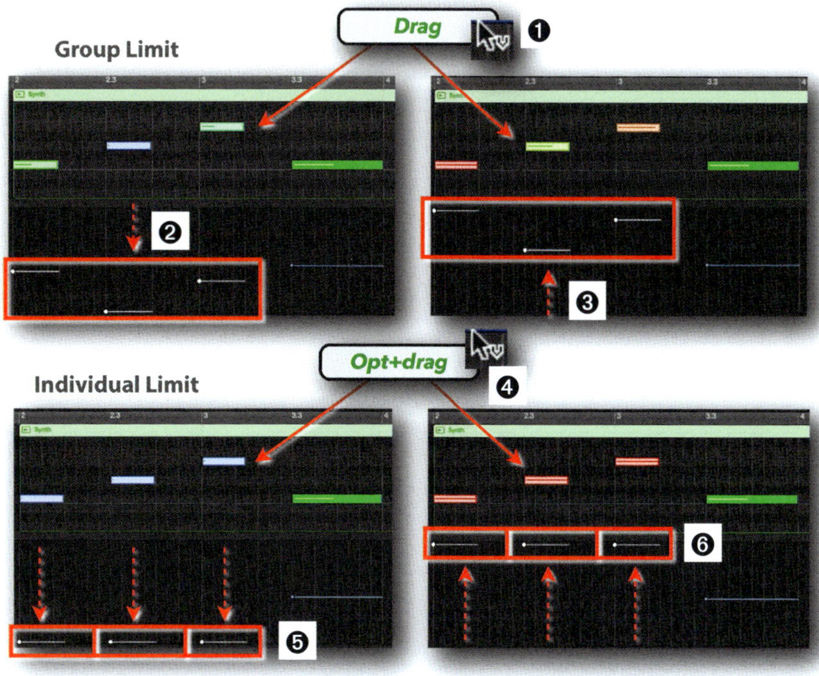
  - ▸ **Operation**: You can change the velocity of a group of MIDI Notes by changing the Cursor Tool to the Velocity Tool ❶ and *click-drag* with it on one of the selected Note Bars up or down.
  - ▸ **Relation between Values**: The velocity values keep their relative values to each other when dragging up or down.
  - ▸ **Limit when moving**:
    - Group Limit: *Dragging* with the Velocity Tool hits the limit when one velocity value of the group reaches its minimum ❷ or maximum value ❸.
    - Individual Limits: Holding down the *option* key ❹ **after** you start dragging will lift this max/min limit. Now, the velocity values of all MIDI Notes continue to move towards the minimum ❺ or maximum ❻ value until the value of each Event reaches that level. Please note, if you use the modifier keys *ctr+cmd* to overwrite the current Tool with the Velocity Tool, then you also have to hold down the *option* key **after** you start dragging with the *ctr+cmd* key pressed down.

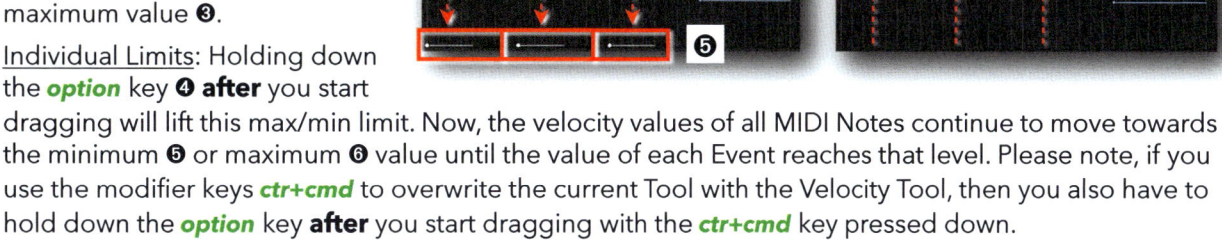

- 🟡 **Local Inspector**
  - ▸ **Operation**: The Velocity Slider displays the value of the note with the lowest velocity value ❼ of a group of selected MIDI Notes. *Dragging* the slider left or right will change the velocity value of all selected Note Events.
  - ▸ **Relation between Values**: The velocity values keep their relative values to each other.
  - ▸ **Limit when moving**:
    - Group Limit: *Dragging* ❽ the slider left/right will move the velocity values up/down until the first value reaches that limit.
    - Individual Limits: Lifting the Limit with the *option* key ❾ seems a bit buggy. You have to hold down the option key first and then move the Velocity Slider, or *opt+click* along the Slider (not the slider knob). The limit will only be lifted on top, but not at the bottom ❿ (strange).

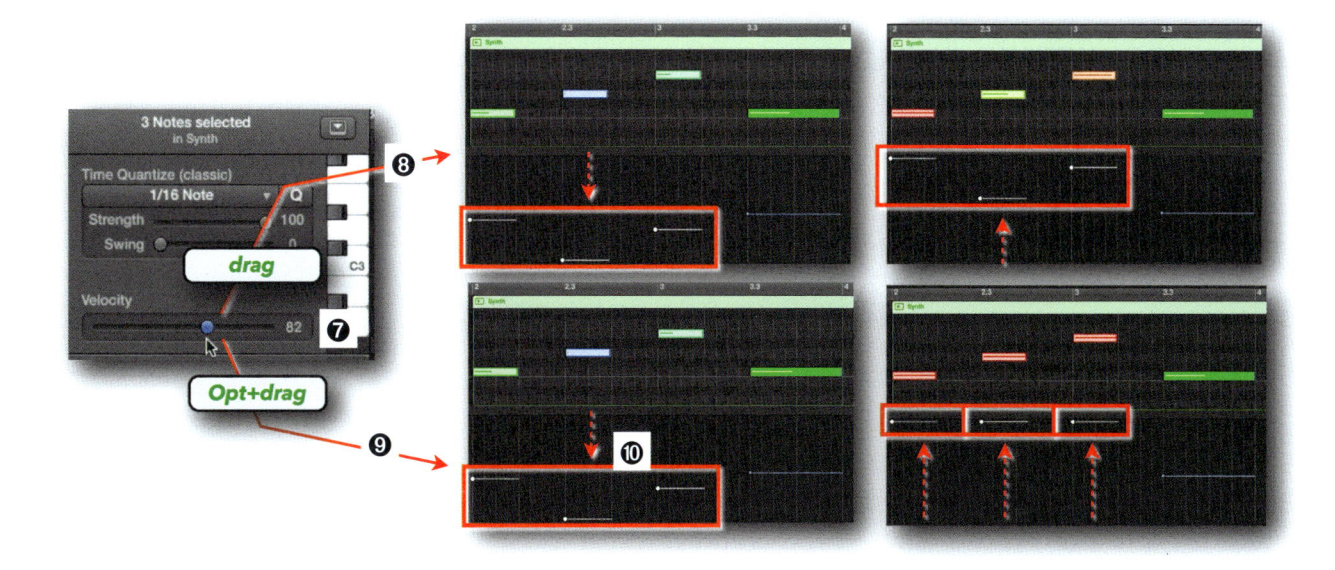

3 - Special Click Actions

MIDI Draw Area

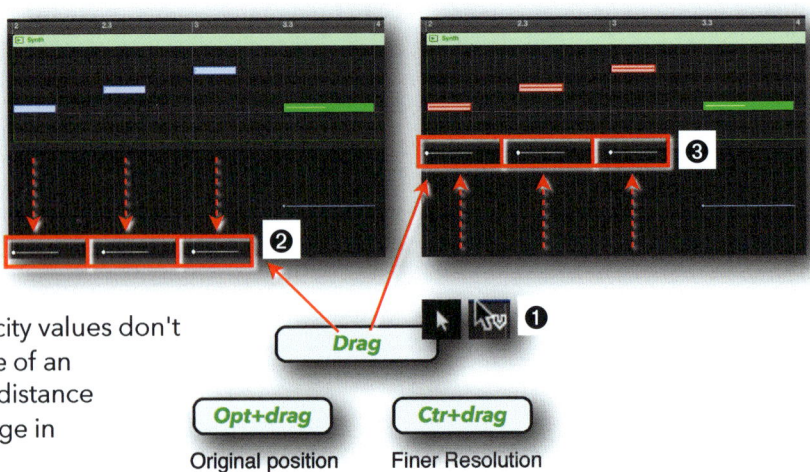

- **Operation**: You can change the velocity values by *dragging* the head of the Velocity Line with the Pointer Tool ❶. Using the Velocity Tool, you can *drag* anywhere in the MIDI Draw Area to move the selected Velocity Lines.
- **Relation between Values**: The velocity values don't change proportionally, it seems more of an exponential change. The bigger the distance between values, the bigger the change in relation to the mouse movement.
- **Limit when moving**:
  - Individual Limit: This time, there is no Group Limit when one value reaches the min or max. Once one value reaches the limit, you can keep on dragging until all values reached the minimum ❷ or maximum ❸ value. Also, when you drag in the opposite direction (after reaching the max/min and without releasing the mouse), the relationship between the values is being re-established.

Please note:
- Holding down the *option* key while *dragging* will temporarily lock the values to the position when you started to drag until you release the option key.
- *Ctr+dragging* will move the velocity values with a finer resolution.

Event List

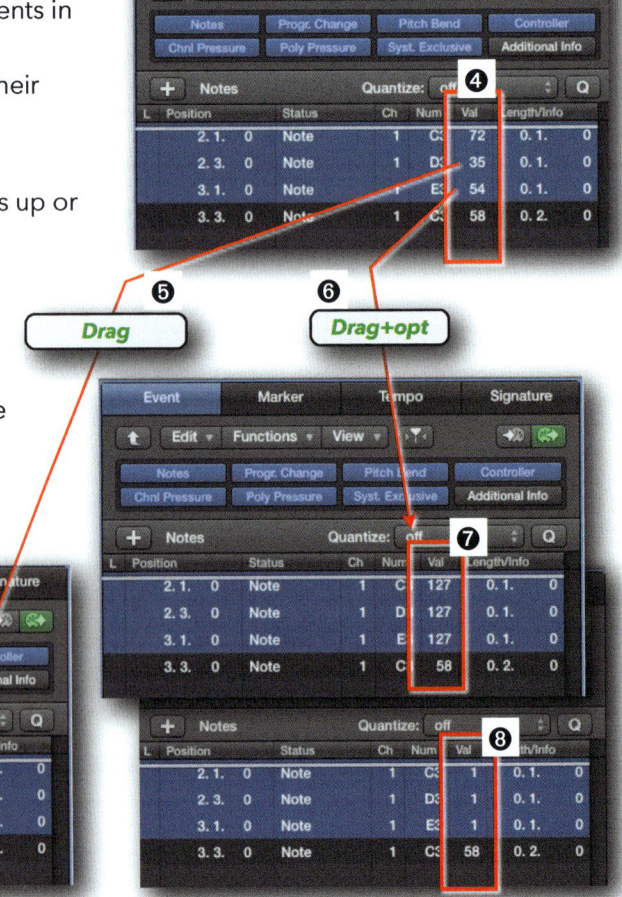

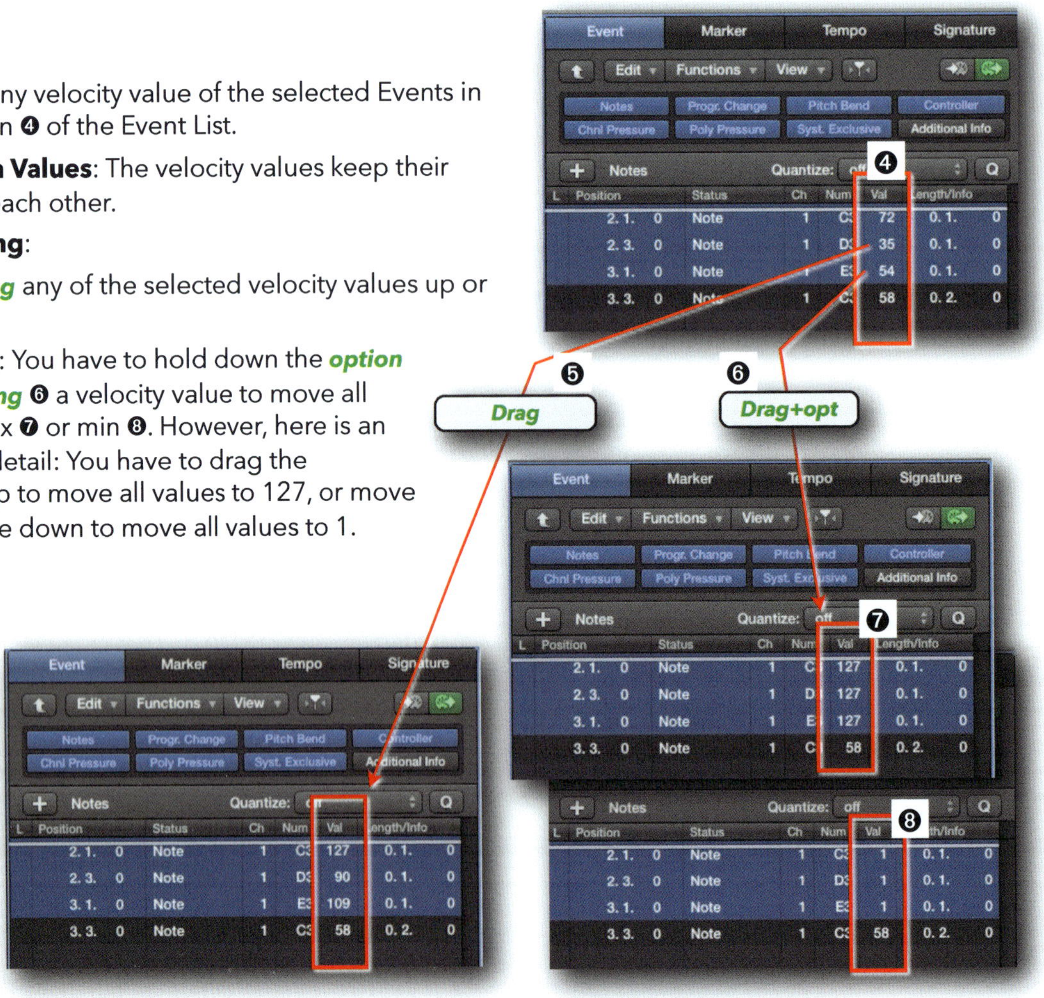

- **Operation**: *Drag* any velocity value of the selected Events in the Velocity column ❹ of the Event List.
- **Relation between Values**: The velocity values keep their relative values to each other.
- **Limit when moving**:
  - Group Limit: *Drag* any of the selected velocity values up or down ❺.
  - Individual Limits: You have to hold down the *option* key **after** *dragging* ❻ a velocity value to move all values to the max ❼ or min ❽. However, here is an important little detail: You have to drag the smallest value up to move all values to 127, or move the biggest value down to move all values to 1.

3 - Special Click Actions

Drag Velocity Ramp in the MIDI Draw Area

➡ Review

Instead of adjusting the velocity values manually, you can use a quick click operation to create a "velocity ramp" for a crescendo or diminuendo.

➡ Attention

The ramps are drawn in the MIDI Draw Area of the Piano Roll Editor (or Score Editor) when Note Velocity is selected.

🔸 Absolute Curve

- You can draw from left to right or right to left, ramp up or ramp down. In this example, I have a sequence of repeating notes with the same velocity values ❶.
- **Click+hold** on a position ❷. Its horizontal coordinate defines the start time of the ramp and the vertical coordinate defines the velocity value.
- Keep holding down the mouse and drag. A green straight line appears ❸.
- A Help Tag ❹ displays the coordinates of the cursor as you drag along as the "End Position" (horizontal coordinate as time) and Velocity (vertical coordinate).
- The green straight line will be drawn as you drag the ramp, and when you release the mouse, any blue velocity line (representing the velocity value of a note in the range where you drew the line) will be placed along that line ❺.
- Of course, you can undo the action and try again.
- You don't have to draw a ramp, just drawing a parallel line will move all velocity values of those Notes to that value corresponding to that line.

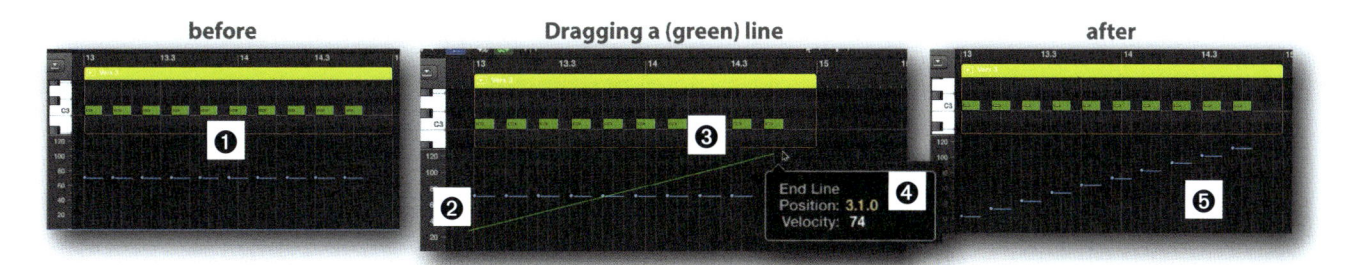

before — **Dragging a (green) line** — **after**

🔸 Time Display

Please pay attention to the Help Tag. The current cursor Position can be displayed in three different ways:

- **Musical Time ❻**: If you have enabled "*Use musical grid*" ❾ for your Project Type in *Project Settings ➤ General* or Main Menu *Record ➤ Use Musical Grid*, then the Help Tag will display bars and beats ❻.
- **Absolute Time ❼**: If you've deselected "*Use musical grid*" for your Project Type, then the Help Tag will display SMPTE time ❼.
- **Musical and Absolute Time ❽**: If you have the Secondary Ruler enabled ❿ (Local View Menu), then both times will be displayed in the Help Tag ❽.

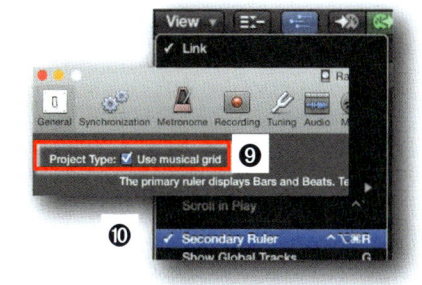

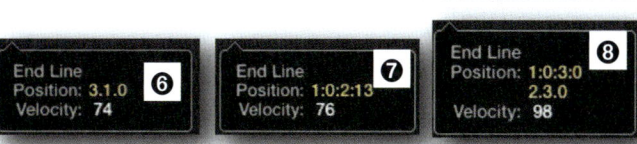

3 - Special Click Actions   57

Offset Curve (Scale)

There is a variation for the "drawing a velocity ramp" procedure, and it's called *Scaling*. The procedure is the same (just holding down a modifier key), but the effect is completely different.

- ▸ Holding down the **command** key ❶ while **dragging** the line, switches the operation to Scale.
- ▸ The Help Tag displays "Scale Position" ❷ instead of "End Position".
- ▸ You can hold down the command key or release it while you are dragging. The important part is the key has to be pressed when you release the mouse.
- ▸ This time, the line you draw in Scale Mode does not overwrite existing velocity values with new absolute velocity values based on the vertical position of the line. Instead, the line applies an offset value to the existing velocity values you draw over. Here is how it works:
    - The first click position ❸ has an offset of zero. It just defines the start point of an invisible reference line ❹.
    - When you draw a line ❺ (in either direction), think of it as the math function "y=x+n" (in case you paid attention in math class).
    - The distance between the Reference Line and the Dragged Line defines the offset value ❻ that is applied to the existing velocity value at any given point along the time axis.
    - In math terms, the bigger the value "n" (the steeper the curve), the bigger the increase of the offset values along the line. A positive n-value (line goes up), will add increasing values to the existing velocity values and a negative n-value (line goes down), will decrease the existing velocity values more and more. 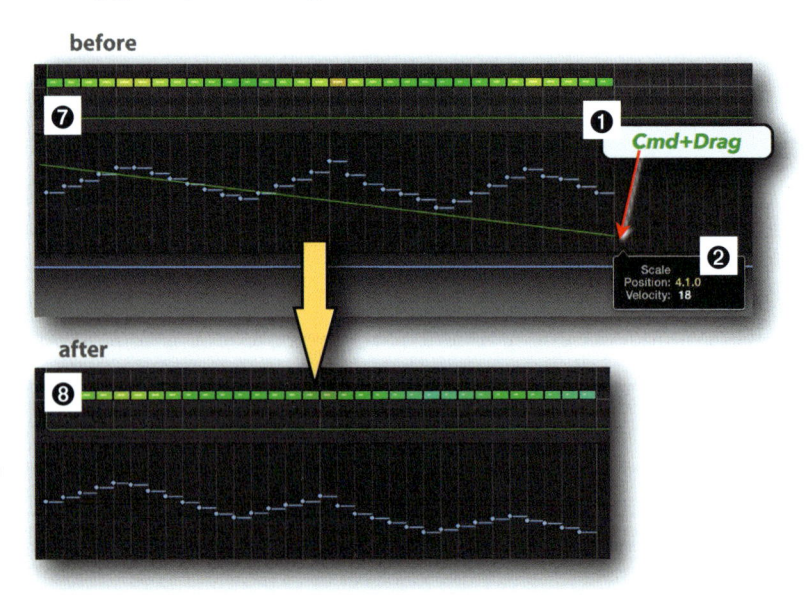
- ▸ Here is an example that shows the effect. A sequence of notes increases and decreases in velocity (like a slow Tremolo effect) ❼. When applying a scale to that ❶, the values become lower and lower while keeping the overall "shape" of the change in value ❽.

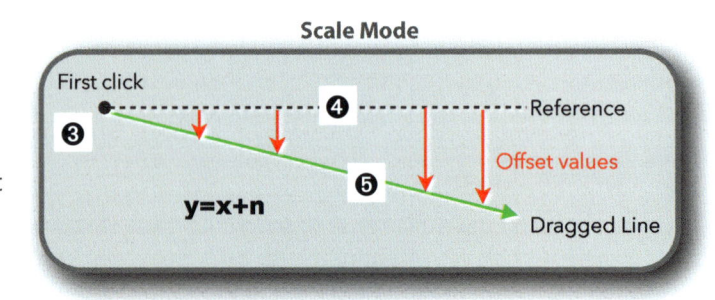

Scale and Select

This is another variation. Holding down the **option** and **command** key switches the Help Tag to display "*Scale and Select Position*" ❾. However, I couldn't find any information about what that is or what it does.

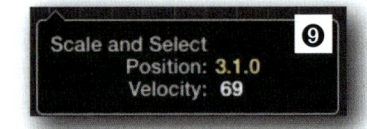

Other Select Actions

- ▸ **Sh+drag** in the MIDI Draw Area will select all the Velocity Lines (or Control Points) along the drawn time axis.
- ▸ **Opt+click** on the MIDI Draw Area will select all the Velocity Lines (or Control Points) from the click position to the end of the Region.

Special Pencil Tool Functionality

➡ Review

The Pencil Tool is one of the more often used tools when editing in Logic. In addition to creating new Note Events (or Control Points and Regions), it has many more functions.

➡ Attention

First, here is a list of different methods on how to switch to the Pencil Tool:
- Select it from the Tool Menu ❶
- Select it in the "Command-click Tool Menu" ❷ to use with a *cmd+click*
- Select it in the "Control-click Tool Menu" ❸ to use with the *ctr+click*
- Use the Key Command (*Set Pencil Tool*) **unassigned** ❹
- To quickly switch to the Pencil Tool, hit the key *T* and then the key *2*. To revert back to the Pointer Tool, hit the key *T* twice. The Key Command *T* opens a special Floating Tool Menu ❺. Here, each Tool has a fixed key assigned to it, the key *2* for the Pencil Tool and the key *T* for the Pointer Tool

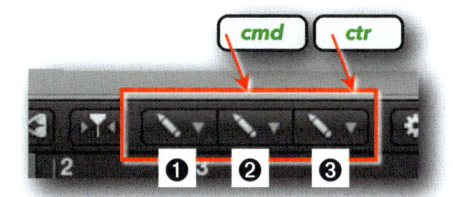

✦ Pencil Functions

These are the different functions for the Pencil Tool in the Piano Roll:

▶ **Create**: *Click* on an empty area ❻ on the Note Area to create a new Note Event.
  - The note length is determined by the value of the current Default Note (16th note or last value of the last selected note).
  - The Velocity is determined by the current position of the Velocity Slider in the Local Inspector ❼.
  - After the click, the Pencil Tool changes to the Resize Tool ❽, because the cursor is positioned at a Click Zone (the left border of a note).

▶ **Create + change length**: *Click-drag* creates a new note at the click position and lets you resize the length by dragging left-right until you release the mouse. This length becomes the new Default Note.

▶ **Create with "Quantize" Note Length**: *Sh+click* creates a note using the current Quantize value ❾ in the Local Inspector as the note length value.

▶ **Create Sequence of Notes**: *Sh+drag* has the same function as the Brush Tool. It creates a sequence of notes with the length that is defined in the Time Quantize ❾ of the Local Inspector.

▶ **Delete**: *Double+click* on an existing Note Event to delete that note.

▶ **Move**: *Drag* on an existing Note Event to move that note.

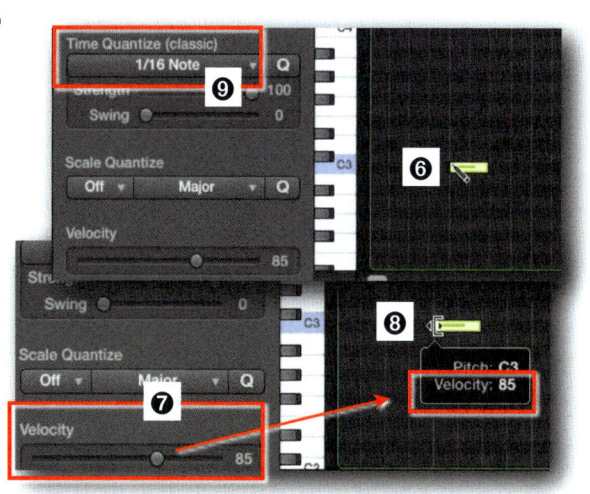

3 - Special Click Actions

Open Score Editor or Event Float from Piano Roll

➡ Review

There are plenty of commands to open specific Editor Windows, but there are also some commands to open Editor Windows from inside other Editor Windows.

➡ Attention

- ▸ In the Piano Roll (either the window pane or standalone window), *double-click* on a Note Event ❶ to open the Event Float.
- ▸ In the Piano Roll (either the window pane or standalone window), *opt-double-click* on a Note Event ❷ to open the Score Editor as a standalone window with that note selected.
- ▸ In the Score Editor, *opt+double-click* on a Note Event ❸ to open the Event List as a standalone window with that note selected.

Opt+Scroll to Zoom horizontally and vertically

To quickly zoom in and out when editing in the Piano Roll you can use the two Zoom Sliders in the upper right corner. Please note that instead of moving those tiny sliders, it is much easier to move them with the following commands:

- ❹ Moving the vertical Zoom Slider is the same as *opt+scrolling horizontally* with your mouse or trackpad

- ❺ Moving the horizontal Zoom Slider is the same as *opt+scrolling vertically* with your mouse or trackpad

3 - Special Click Actions

Workflow

Show a Specific Menu Command in the Key Commands Window

➡ **Review**

Here is a quick review on the Menu Commands:

- ▸ Menu Commands are available in the Main Menu ❶ and also in the individual Local Menus ❷ of many Window Panes or standalone Windows. 
- ▸ Keep in mind that those Menus are often dynamic, which means, the available commands displayed in those menus can change based on various circumstances. Especially the Edit Menu, which changes quite a bit depending on what type of object is selected.
- ▸ Most of the Menu Commands are also available as Key Commands.
- ▸ If a Menu Command is assigned to a Key Command ❸, then the key combination is listed next to the command.
- ▸ Most of the Key Commands can be reassigned ❹ in the Key Commands Window with a few exceptions. Those "reserved" key combinations (mostly OSX system-wide Key Commands) are grayed out ❺.

There is one hidden command that comes in handy if you want to assign or re-assign a Menu Command to a different Key combination.

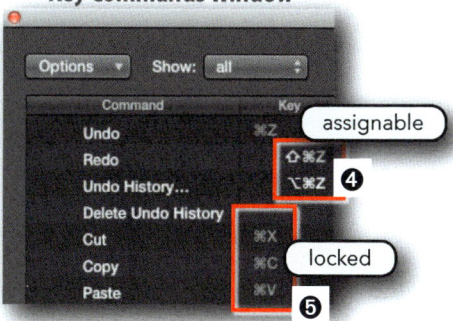

➡ **Attention**

If you open a menu and see a command that doesn't have a Key Command assignment and you want to assign one to it, or you want to change the currently assigned key combination, then you have to open the Key Command Window ❻, search for that Key Command, and do the assignment. However, there is a faster way.

Hold down the *control* key while *clicking* on a command in the open Menu ❼ and the Key Commands Window will automatically open with that command already selected (you might scroll up or down a bit depending on the current window size). Now, assign the key combination and you are done.

Double-Arrow Playhead Position Tool

➡ **Review**

◁▷ Let's look at a special Cursor Tool that is not available in the Tool Menu, the one with the double arrow symbol. Let's call it the **Playhead Position Tool**. It has many functions and some exceptions you have to be aware of.

➡ **Attention**

First, a quick look at the Ruler. The Ruler area displays actually two Rulers by default:
- ▶ **Primary Ruler ❶**: This is the area that displays the time units as Musical Time (bar/beats) or Absolute Time (SMPTE), depending on the Project Type setting (*Project Settings ➤ General*). It also displays the Cycle Range.
- ▶ **Playhead Ruler ❷**: The Playhead Ruler has multiple functionalities:
  - It shows time divisions as little lines that extend into vertical grid lines depending on the zoom factor.
  - It displays the so-called *Playhead Thumb* ❸, the top of the Playhead, as a gray triangle.
  - When you move the Cursor Tool over the Playhead Ruler, it changes to the double-arrow Playhead Position Tool ❹ ◁▷.
  - You can *click* or *drag* on the Playhead Ruler with the Playhead Position Tool to position the Playhead.
  - *Ctr+click* on the Playhead Ruler to open the Ruler-specific Shortcut Menu.
  - *Opt+cmd+click* on the Playhead Ruler to toggle the Autopunch Ruler.

The click and drag actions with the Playhead Position Tool along the Playhead Ruler are slightly different on the various time-based windows, the ones that have a Ruler (Tracks Window, Piano Roll, etc.). First, I like to introduce the four main click actions with the Playhead Position Tool ◁▷ and then show you how they function or function differently in the various time-based windows.

1. **Click** on the Playhead Ruler ❺: This is the action where you click anywhere along the Playhead Ruler to position the Playhead.
2. **Drag** on the Playhead Ruler ❻: This is the action where you click-drag anywhere along the Playhead Ruler to position the Playhead by sliding it along the Ruler.
3. **Drag** the Playhead Thumb ❼: This is the action where you click-hold on the Playhead Thumb and drag it along to re-position it.
4. **Drag** the Playhead Line ❽: This is the action where you click-hold anywhere on the vertical Playhead line, not the thumb to reposition it.

Attention Please note that the dragging motion of the Playhead follows an underlying smart grid (depending on the zoom level). *Ctr+drag* will disable that grid and lets you drag in a finer resolution.

3 - Special Click Actions

◉ Tracks Window

All four actions with the Playhead Position Tool ◀▶ work as aspected in the Tracks Window.
- ▸ You can *click* and *drag* along the Playhead Ruler and the double-arrow Playhead Position Tool always indicates that you are controlling the Playhead Position.
- ▸ There is one special feature called **Scrubbing** that changes the effect of the Playhead Position Tool. 
  - When in Pause Mode ❶ (clicking the Pause Button), *dragging* the Playhead with the Playhead Position Tool will play back the Project based on the speed you are moving the Playhead, to the right (plays forward) or left (plays backwards).
  - This Scrubbing feature is automatically enabled for MIDI Regions and Drummer Regions, but has to be enabled for Audio Regions in the *Preferences ➤ Audio ➤ Editing* ❷.

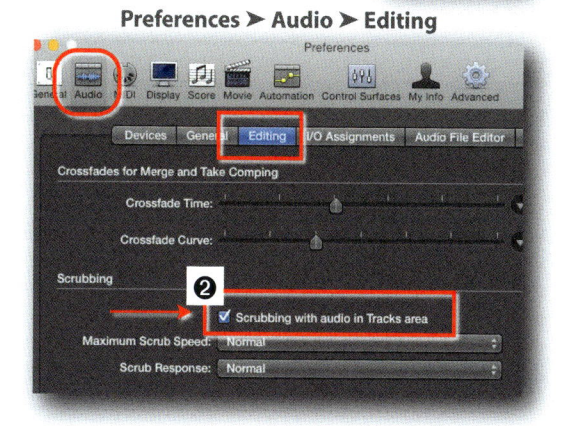

◉ Audio Track Editor

All the actions with the Playhead Position Tool work in the Audio Track Editor, even Scrubbing when in Pause Mode.

However, there is one exception:
- ▸ You can't *drag* the vertical Playhead Line. You will notice that the Cursor doesn't change to the Playhead Position Tool. Dragging on the line is the same as dragging on the Region itself, which will move the Region ❸ on the timeline.

◉ Score Editor

All the actions with the Playhead Position Tool work in the Score Editor, as well as Scrubbing, when in Pause Mode. There is one specialty:
- ▸ The Score Editor has three different Views, some of them don't have a Ruler on top. In that case, there is a special functionality. Holding down the *option* key when hovering over a staff changes the cursor to the Playhead Position Tool ◀▶ ❹. Now you can drag the Playhead along the staff like you would on the Playhead Ruler.

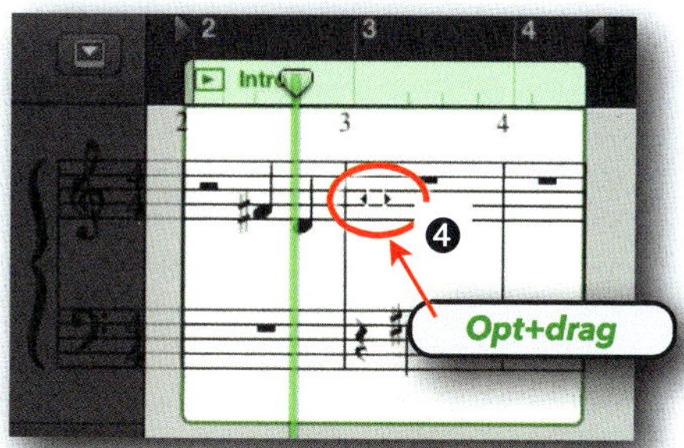

◉ Piano Roll Editor

The Piano Roll also needs attention for some exceptions:
- ▸ The Region Header ❺ in the Piano Roll is displayed on top of the Playhead Ruler. This area is reserved for repositioning the Region. You will notice that the cursor is displaying the Pointer Tool ❻ when you hover over a Region Header. It is not changing to the Playhead Position Tool. Therefore, *dragging* along the Region Header will move the Region and not the Playhead.
- ▸ However, you can click on the Region Header to position the Playhead there. Once the cursor is positioned over the Playhead Thumb ❼, it changes to the Playhead Position Tool ◀▶ and you can drag it, even across the Region Header.
- ▸ Dragging the Playhead Line is also not possible in the Piano Roll.

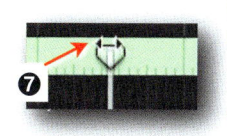

3 - Special Click Actions

Three Tools - Four Tool Menus

➡ Review

The default mouse cursor is the Pointer Tool, n Logic and virtually any other app. To perform specific graphic oriented tasks, apps can switch to different Tools with specific symbols to indicate what tool it is.

In Logic, you can switch the Tools in three different ways

- ▶ **Automatic**: Moving the Cursor Tool over a designated area, a so-called Click Zone or hot spot, can automatically switch to a specific Tool. This can speed up the workflow tremendously, because the right Tool is automatically selected.
- ▶ **Modifier Keys**: Holding down modifier keys might change the Tool.
- ▶ **Key Command**: Most of the Cursor Tools can be selected by using their corresponding Key Command.
- ▶ **Tool Menu**: Many windows have a Tool Menu where you can select the right Tool for the task.

➡ Attention

Please keep in mind that the basic functionality of the Tool Menu is the same for different windows (Tracks Window, Piano Roll, etc.), they just have a different set of tools, appropriate for those tasks.

Three different Tools

You can pre-select up to three different Tools:

- ▶ **Main Tool ❶**: This is the Tool that you use with your mouse when you click or drag around the windows.
- ▶ **Command-click Tool ❷**: This Tool is only active when you hold down the *command* key. This way you can quickly switch to that secondary Tool by just holding down that modifier key.
- ▶ **Control-click Tool ❸**: This Tool is only active when you hold down the *control* key. This way you can quickly switch to a third Tool by just holding down that modifier key.

Select a Tool

You simply select a Tool by clicking on one of the three Tool Menu Buttons to open its Tool Menu and select the Tool for the Main Tool ❶, the Command-click Tool ❷, or the Control-click Tool ❸.

Overwrite Tools

Please note that whatever Tool is selected, it can temporarily be overwritten under the following circumstances:

- ▶ The selected Tool is only active inside a specific window. Moving the cursor over a different window or window pane (i.e., from the Tracks Window to the Piano Roll), changes to the Tool that is selected in that window.
- ▶ The selected Tool is only visible in the area of the window where it has functionality. If not, then it defaults back to the Pointer Tool.
- ▶ A Click Zone or a specific key combination can overwrite the Tool and change temporarily to a different Tool.

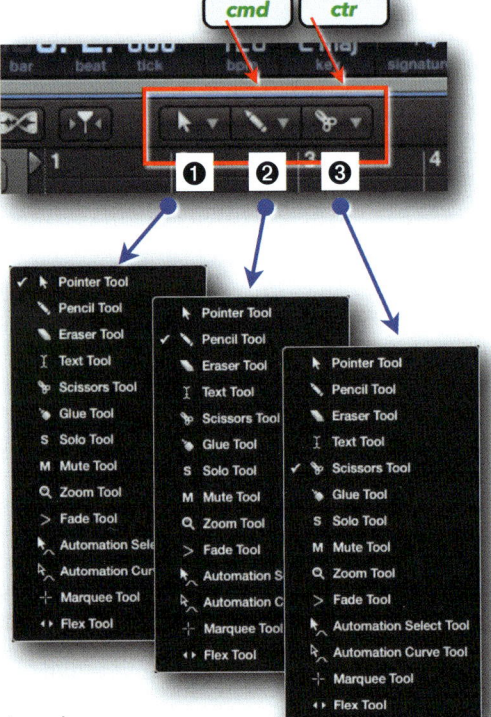

Third Tool (optional)

The third Tool (Control-click Tool) is not available by default. Its functionality has to be enabled.

▶ In the *Preferences ➤ General ➤ Editing ➤ Right Mouse Button* select "Is *Assignable to a Tool*" from the popup menu ❶.

▶ This places the third Tool Menu Button ❷ on the Menu Bar.

▶ When enabled, the third button will be available in all windows that have a Tool Menu.

Free-floating Main Tool Menu

The Tool Menu ❸ for any of the three types of Tools opens by *clicking* on any of the Tool Menu Buttons ❹. However, there is a special Tool Menu that also lets you select the Main Tool. It functions as a free-floating Menu that can be displayed in three ways:

▶ **Open the Menu**

📌 In the *Preferences ➤ General ➤ Editing ➤ Right Mouse Button* select "Opens Tool Menu" ❺. Now the free-floating Tool Menu pops up when you *ctr+click* on the window.

📌 In the *Preferences ➤ General ➤ Editing ➤ Right Mouse Button* select "Opens Tool and Shortcut Menu" ❻. Now the free-floating Tool Menu is added to the Shortcut Menu that pops up when you *ctr+click* on the window.

📌 Use the Key Command (*Show Tool Menu*) *T*. This pops up the same menu ❺.

▶ **Functionality:** The free-floating Tool Menu is different from the standard Tool Menu (that you open by clicking on the Tool Menu Button), because it has numbers and letters assigned next to each Tool ❼. They function as "temporary" Key Commands that have priority over the standard Key Commands assigned to those numbers and letters as long the free-floating window is open. Now, instead of selecting a Tool with the mouse, you can type the corresponding Key Command which selects that Tool and closes the menu.

You may notice that the Pointer Tool has the Key Command *T* assigned to it. This provides a very fast procedure to revert back to the Pointer Tool when a different Tool is currently selected. Just hit the key *T* twice. The first keystroke opens the floating Tool Menu and the second key stroke selects the Pointer Tool and automatically closes the free-floating Tool Menu.

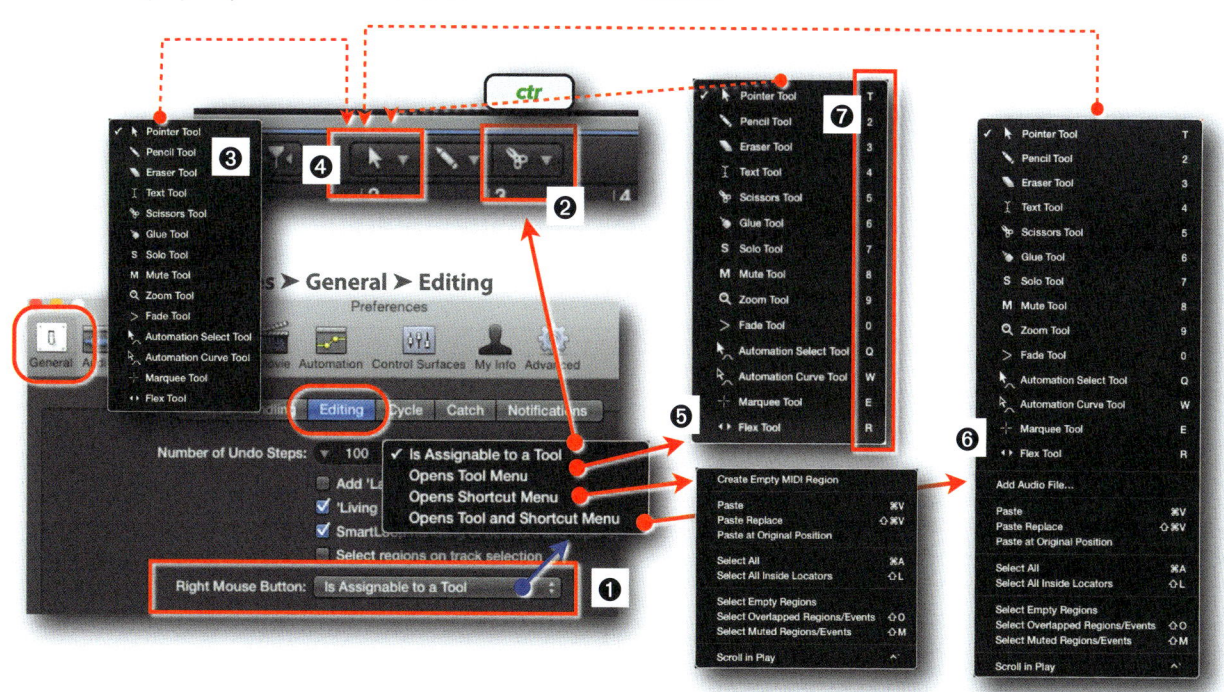

The selected Tools are saved with Screensets. This lets you create different Screensets not only to pre-configure specific window arrangements, but also switch between specific Tool Selections.

3 - Special Click Actions

Key Equivalents for Non-Extended Keyboards

➡ **Review**

An Extended Keyboard has a middle section ❶ and the number keypad ❷ with special keys. Those special keys are missing ❸ on the smaller size wireless keyboard or the keyboard on a laptop. However, if those keys are assigned to Key Commands in Logic, you still have a chance to use them.

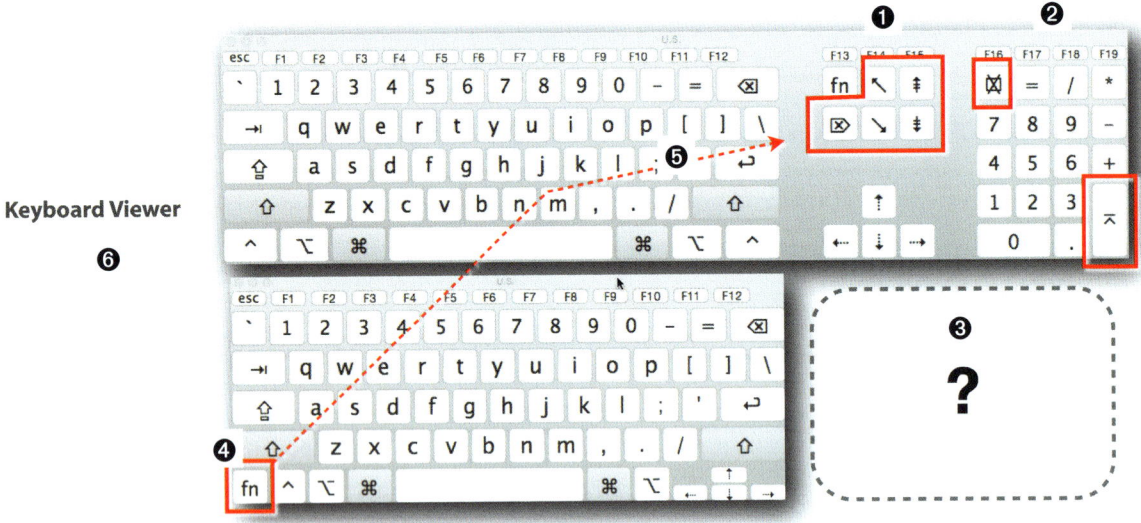

Keyboard Viewer ❻

➡ **Attention**

Apple keyboards have a special function key `fn` ❹ that you can use as a modifier key to access the missing keys ❺ of an Extended Keyboard.

Special Key	Substitute (symbol)	Substitute (name)
home ↖	↖: fn + ←	home: fn + ArrowLeft
end ↘	↘: fn + →	end: fn + ArrowRight
page up ⇞	⇞: fn + ↑	page up: fn + ArrowUp
page down ⇟	⇟: fn + ↓	page down: fn + ArrowDown
enter ⌤	⌤: fn + ↵	enter: fn + return
Forward Delete ⌦	⌦: fn + ⌫	Forward delete: fn + Backward delete

🎧 Keyboard Viewer

Anytime you have questions about key assignments on your keyboard, you can use the Keyboard Viewer ❻, a little OSX floating window, that shows your keyboard layout and reacts to any modifier key to show the key assignments (also useful for finding foreign characters or symbols).

In the **System Preferences ➤ Keyboard**, enable the checkbox "*Show Keyboard & Character Viewers in menu bar*" ❼. This places the command "Show/Hide Keyboard Viewer" ❽ under the Menu Extra "Country Flag" ❾ in the Menu Bar.

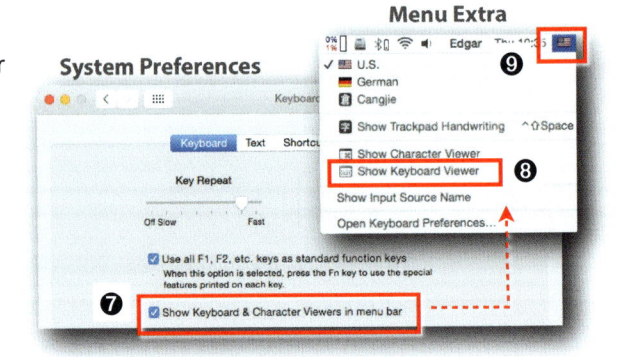

System Preferences

Menu Extra

3 - Special Click Actions

Use Arrow Keys in New Tracks Dialog

➡ *Review*

You open the New Tracks Dialog to select a Track or multiple Tracks. You can directly *double-click* on one of the icons or the buttons if you use the display without icons (*Preferences* ➤ *Display* ➤ *General* ➤ *"Show icons in New Tracks dialog"*). This chooses that Track with the current settings in the Details section and closes the window. If you want to toggle through the icons first, you can use a Key Command to speed things up.

➡ *Attention*

Once the New Tracks Dialog opens, one of the Tracks is already selected (the one that you selected the last time you opened the window). To quickly toggle through the icons or buttons without the mouse, just use the ArrowLeft or ArrowRight key on your keyboard. Once you've selected the Track you wanted, there is no need to grab your mouse, move it over the "Create" button and click on it. Your hands are already on the keyboard using the arrow keys, so just hit the "enter" key and you are done. Less travel time with the mouse.

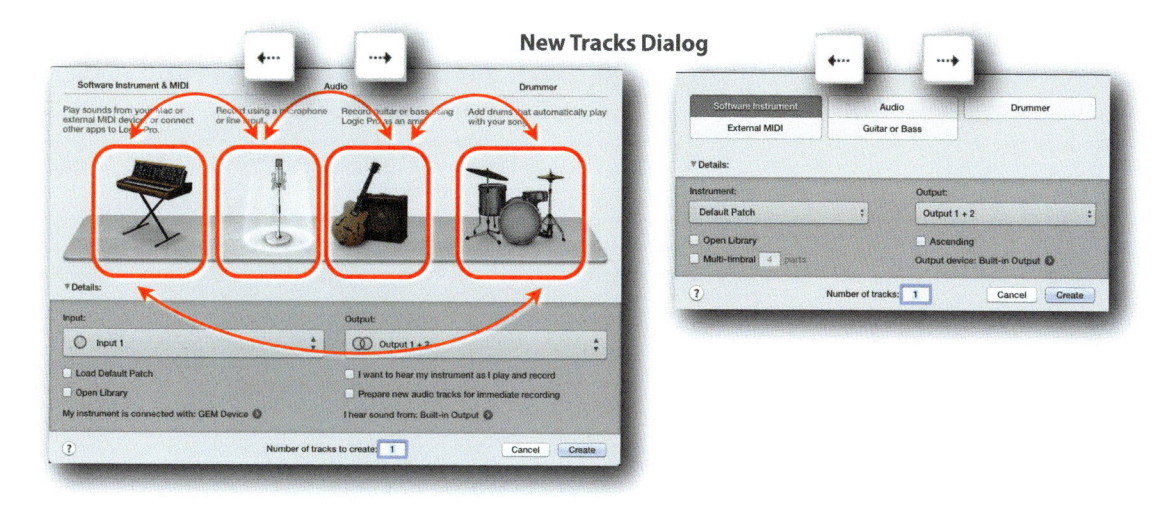

Use OSX Key Commands for Dialog Windows

➡ *Review*

Another opportunity to improve your workflow by cutting down on "mouse-travel time" and use Key Commands instead is when responding to Dialog windows (which also works in other apps).

➡ *Attention*

A Dialog Window often has multiple buttons to make a selection. However, instead of clicking with the mouse on those buttons, most of them have Key Command equivalents, so you can just hit a key instead:

- **Blue (highlighted) Button**: Use the return key for the highlighted buttons.
- **Cancel**: Use the esc key for the Cancel button.
- **Other Buttons**: Any other button is most likely assigned to the key of the first letter of the name on the button. For example " **R**eplace", " **D**on't Close ". Just hit that key together with the *command* key.

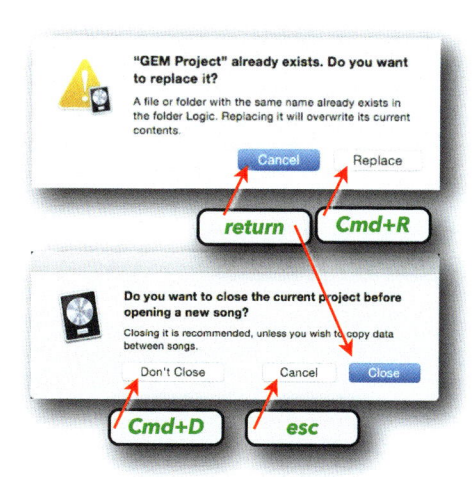

Full Screen Mode vs. "Almost" Full Screen Mode

➡ Review

There are two types of apps when it comes to the use of windows in an app:
- **Multiple Windows**: Many, especially more professional apps, have a multitude of windows for different functionalities and tasks. This requires some sort of window management or "discipline" when opening and closing the windows, so they don't create a cluttered mess on your screen.
- **Single Window**: These types of apps provide a Main Window that lets you perform most of the tasks. Other windows that you need can be shown/hidden as so-called window panes "inside". These areas inside that Main Window let you focus on one "workspace". Only a few windows that you might occasionally need can be opened as a separate standalone window. Apple is moving more apps in recent years towards this type of approach.

LPX is also a Single Window app, providing the Logic Main Window with its numerous window panes and allowing you to work mainly in that one window. You still have the option to use standalone windows.

One advantage of a Single Window app is that you can use Full Screen Mode, which uses the entire screen for that window, blending out everything else, including the Main Menu and the Window Title Bar on top. However, the implementation on how to use Full Screen Mode changed a lot with recent OSX and Logic updates, and there are still some details you have to pay attention to.

➡ Attention

There are three ways to enter and exit Full Screen Mode:
- Menu Command *View ➤ Enter/Exit Full Screen*
- Key Command (*Enter/Exit Full Screen*) ***ctr+cmd+F***
- Use the green Title Bar Button

● Title Bar Buttons

The green button in the upper left corner of a window is one of the three Title Bar Buttons. It is called the Zoom Button (technically it "resizes" a window" rather than "zooming" in or out). The Button can have different appearances to indicate its functionality.

▶ **Full Screen**: Please note that not all windows in Logic have the following functionality:

- Enter Full Screen ❶: As a default, when you move the cursor over the button, it changes to the "Enter Full Screen" button showing two arrows pointing outbound. **Click** on it to switch that window to Full Screen Mode (the Window Title Bar and the Main Menu disappear).

- Exit Full Screen ❷: Once a window is in Full Screen Mode, you have to move the cursor to the top of the screen to make the Menu Bar visible temporarily. Now when you move over that green button, it shows two arrows pointing inwards. **Click** on it to exit Full Screen Mode.

▶ **Zoom Window**: This mode existed in OSX before there was Full Screen Mode. It's still available in many apps under the Main Menu *Window ➤ Zoom* (including Logic). This command (available as Key Command ***ctr+cmd+M***) usually corresponds to the green Title Bar Button. The command resizes the window to its maximum size for the current computer screen. Using it again resizes the window back to its previous size and position. Although the green button is now used for Full Screen Mode, you still can use it in Logic for toggling the Zoom Window command.

- Toggle Zoom Window ❸: Moving the cursor over the green Title Bar Button while holding down the *option* key will switch its functionality to toggle "Zoom Window", displaying a plus inside the button.

Move Windows without Making Them Active Windows

➡ **Review**

Even if you prefer to work in the Main Window and use its Window Panes without the need to open many other windows, you might face situations where you want to see the content in two open windows. If the windows overlap or partially cover each other, then you have to drag and click around to get those windows arranged the way you want it. Here is one little click action that should definitely be a part of your workflow.

➡ **Attention**

The following procedure is a (little known) OSX feature that works with virtually any windows on your computer: **How to move a window without making it an Active Window?**

Here is an example:

- ▸ Let's say you have the Main Window ❶ in the foreground. It is the Active Window indicated by the colored Title Bar Buttons ❷. The second window is the Score Editor ❸, the inactive Window, indicated by the gray Menu Title Buttons ❹.

- ▸ The Inactive Window (Score) is covered by the Active Window (Main Window).

- ▸ Now you want to see the notation of that little phrase that is covered ❺ by the Main Window, so you have to rearrange the windows. Of course, you could move the Main Window down, but let's assume that is not possible. The other option is to move the Score Window (Inactive Window) up.

- ▸ If you go for the second option, then you have to be aware of the "consequences". By *click+dragging* ❻ the Score Window up, you are actually clicking on that window, and therefore, making it the Active Window. You see that those Title Bar Buttons are colored now ❼. However, the previous Active Window (the Main Window) becomes an Inactive Window (gray buttons) ❽ and is covered by the Active Window (Score). That means, it requires another *click* on Logic's Main Window to make it the Active Window again.

- ▸ **Here is the most important rule**: Holding down the *command* key while *dragging* an Inactive Window (Score) ❾ doesn't make it an Active Window. In this example, Logic's Main Window would stay the Active Window (on top) ❿ and you just move the Score Window, the Inactive Window, underneath to arrange it the way you want it.

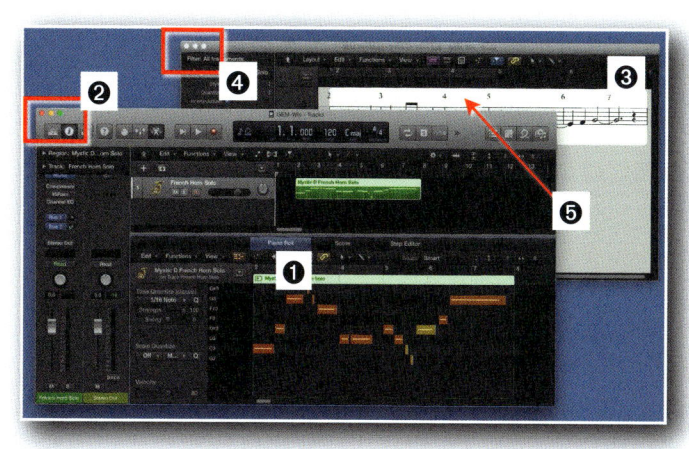

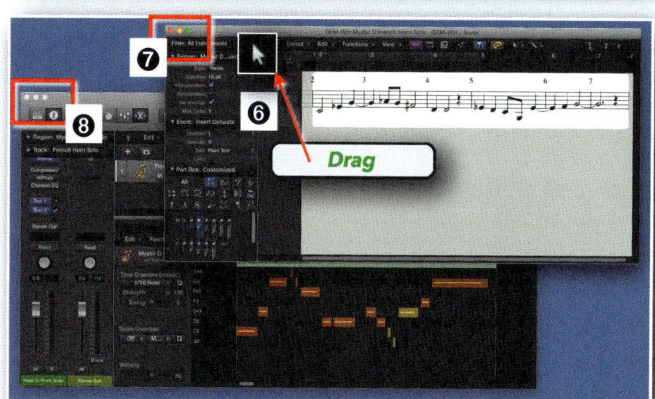

3 - Special Click Actions

4 - Did you Know?

File

Special Proxy Icon Functionality

➡ Review

Learning all the Logic features is already quite a task. However, there are more features that belong to general OSX functionality, but also apply to the general Logic workflow. Chances are, those features are not mentioned in the Logic User Guide or any other Logic book for that matter. Let me introduce to you one of those features - the **Proxy Icon**.

➡ Attention

The Proxy Icon is so small and insignificant that many users might not even be aware that it is there. However, it provides a few nice functions that are worth mentioning. Like many other OSX functions, the following might also apply to other OSX apps:

🌐 Proxy Icon

The Proxy Icon is that little icon in the center of the Window Title Bar, in front of the Project Name.

- ▶ **Appearance**: The Proxy Icon is displayed mainly in Logic's Main Window and is a miniature icon of the actual Logic Project file icon ❶.
- ▶ **Saved - Unsaved**: The icon has two states that correspond to the status of the red Title Bar Button ❷.
    - If the Project is saved (the red Botton is solid 🔴 ❷), then the Proxy Icon is dark ❶.
    - If you made changes to the Project since you last saved it manually (red button now has a dot 🔴 ❸), then the Proxy Icon has a lighter color ❹.
- ▶ **File Path**: *Cmd+click* on the Proxy Icon to open a menu displaying the File Path ❺ where the Project File is stored. Select a folder to open that Finder Window.
- ▶ **Create Project Alias**: *Drag* the Proxy Icon to the Desktop or any other open Finder Window to create an Alias of that Project File. A ghost icon with the alias arrow ❻ tears off while dragging.
- ▶ **Create Project Copy**: *Opt+drag* the Proxy Icon to the Desktop or any other open Finder Window to create a copy of that Project File. A ghost icon with the typical green + symbol ❼ tears off while dragging.

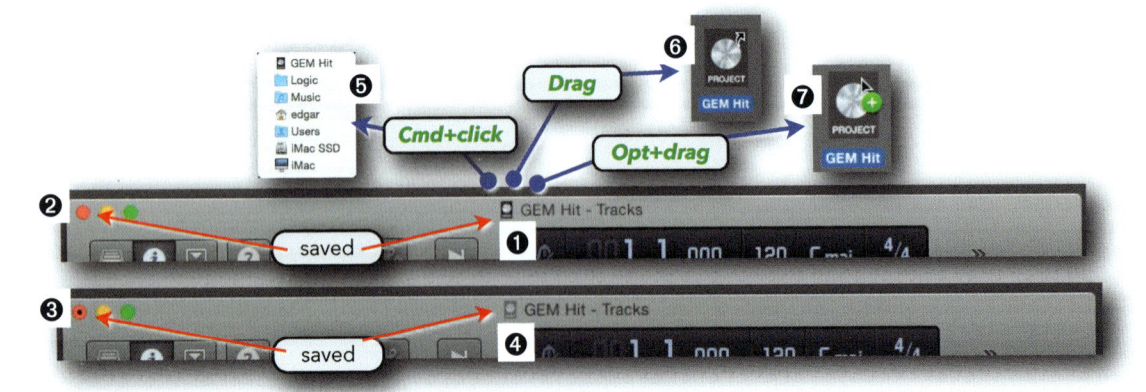

The Alias and Copy function only works when the Project has been saved (dark icon, red button).

Create Loops by Dragging Regions over the Loop Browser

➡ Review

Creating your own Apple Loops is as easy as selecting your Audio Region or MIDI Region in your Project and choosing the Menu Command **File ➤ Export ➤ "Region to Loop Library..."** ❶, or using its corresponding Key Command **sh+ctr +O**, which opens the Dialog Window ❷ to enter the Meta Data for the Loop. But there is an even easier way to do it.

➡ Attention

Drag the Region ❸ directly from the Track Lane onto the open Loop Browser ❹. This will also open the Dialog Window ❷ to create the new Apple Loop.

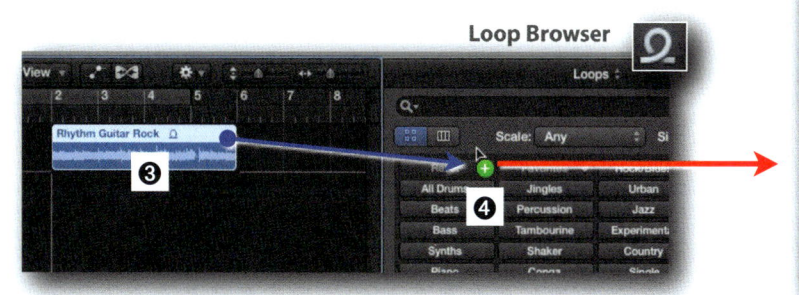

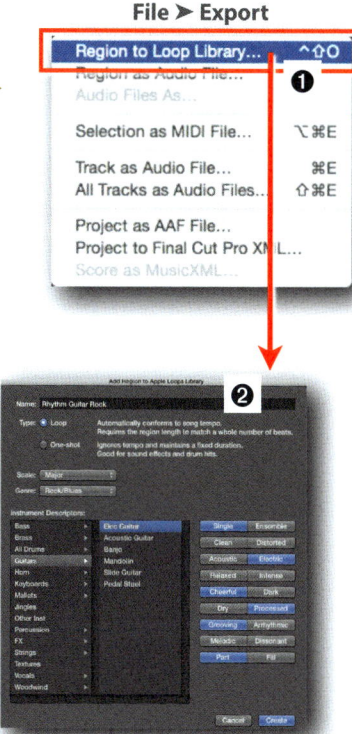

Delete Backup Files inside a Project

➡ Review

Every time you save a Project, Logic automatically backs up the previously saved version of your Project, so you can revert to that previous version is case you messed up.

The **Preferences ➤ General ➤ Project Handling ➤ Auto Backup** settings ❺ lets you choose how many backups Logic keeps, between 0 and 100. The saved backups are listed in the Menu **File ➤ Revert to ➤** ❻ with their corresponding time stamp. You just select one to load that backup.

➡ Attention

Selecting "Off" from the Auto Backup settings will delete all the Backups next time you save your Project. This is the same effect as selecting "Delete Backups" from the **File ➤ Project Management ➤ Clean Up...** ❽ .

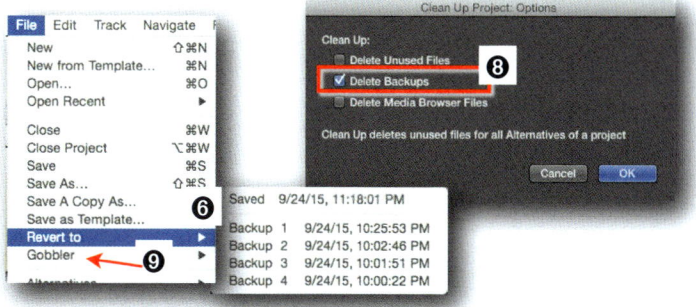

Make sure to check out the new chapter in my book "Logic Pro X - The Details" to learn how to setup iCloud backups using Gobbler ❾.

4 - Did you Know?   71

Tracks Window

Logic in GarageBand Mode

➡ *Review*

GarageBand 10 and Logic Pro X share the same code base, which means, it is basically one app, optimizing the further development of both apps. The developer "just" disable (hide) the more advanced features of Logic in the code and release it as GarageBand.

This also has the major advantage for the users who started with GarageBand and want to upgrade to Logic. They don't have to learn a new app, everything is pretty much the same, just with more features.

➡ *Attention*

To make the transition process from GarageBand to Logic even more easier, Logic has an Advanced Preferences page ❶ that lets you show/hide specific advanced features (Score, Surround, Advanced Editing, etc.). If you disable the main checkbox "**Show Advanced Tools**"❷, then Logic will not only hide the advanced tool, it will also change some GUI (graphical user interface) elements to make it look like GarageBand, for example, the wooden GarageBand panels ❸ on the side and even exchanges the buttons on the Track Header ❹ with the ones used in GarageBand ❺.

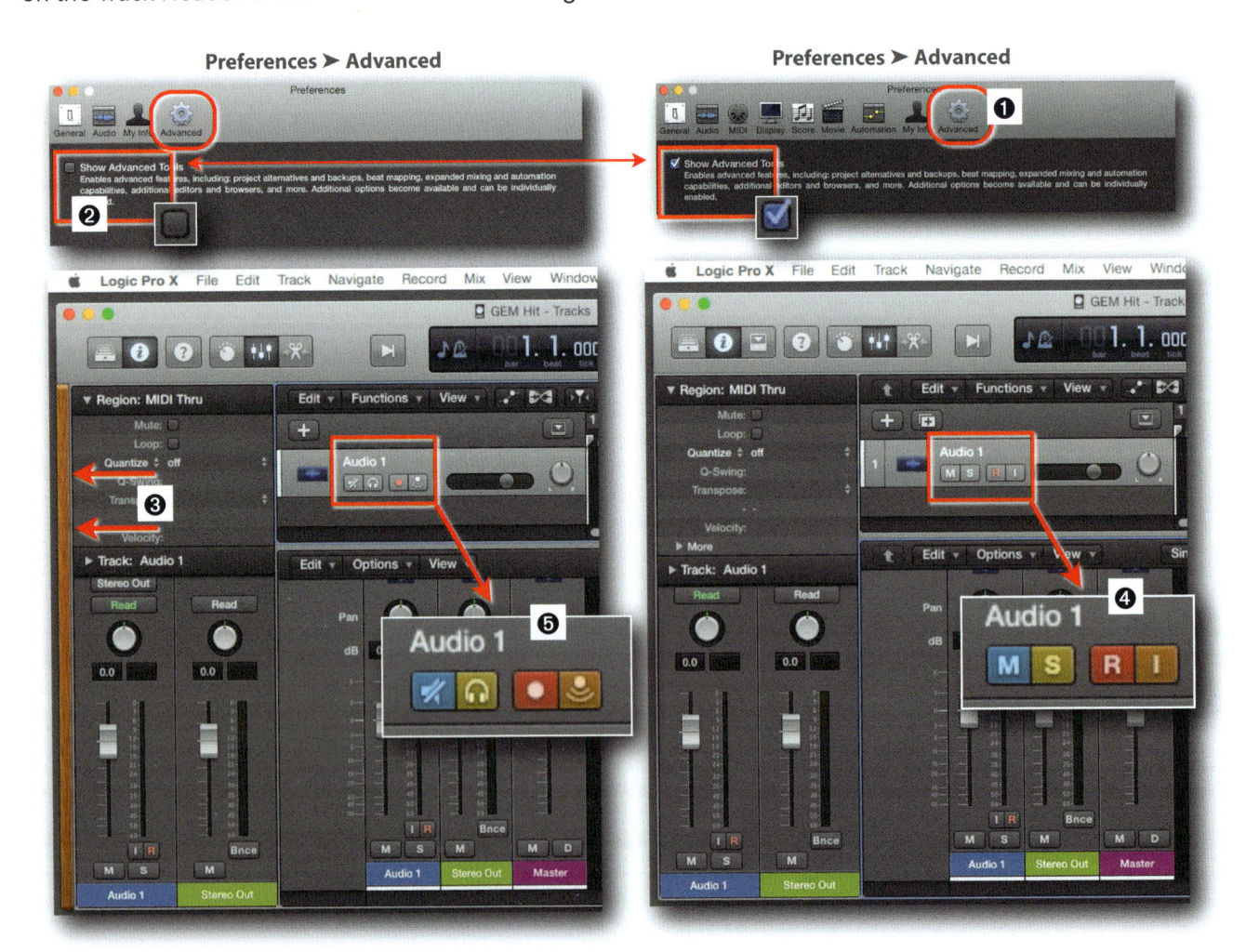

Batch-rename Regions Sequentially

➡ Review

The following is an old feature that has existed in Logic for a long time, but still, many Logic users are not aware of it. It is about batch naming Regions.

➡ Attention

Logic provides many different ways to rename Regions.

💡 Naming Single Region

You can rename Regions in the following places:

- **Region Inspector ❶**: Select the Region in the Workspace and *double-click* on its name in the Header of the Region Inspector. Enter the new name in the blue entry field that appears.
- **Track Lane ❷**: *Click* on the Region with the Text Tool.
- **Track Editor ❸**: *Click* on the Region with the Text Tool. MIDI Regions cannot be renamed in the MIDI Editors.
- **Project Audio Browser ❹**: *Double-click* on the Region Name to enter a new one in the blue entry field.

💡 Naming Multiple Regions

To rename multiple Regions with the same name, just select all the Regions first and use the same naming procedure. Please note that in the Project Audio Browser, you can only name one Region at a time.

💡 Naming Multiple Regions Sequentially

If you use any of the procedures (except Project Audio Browser) and type in a name, followed by a space, and a number, then Logic renames all the selected Regions sequentially from left to right (even across multiple Tracks), counting up the numbers, starting with the number you entered.

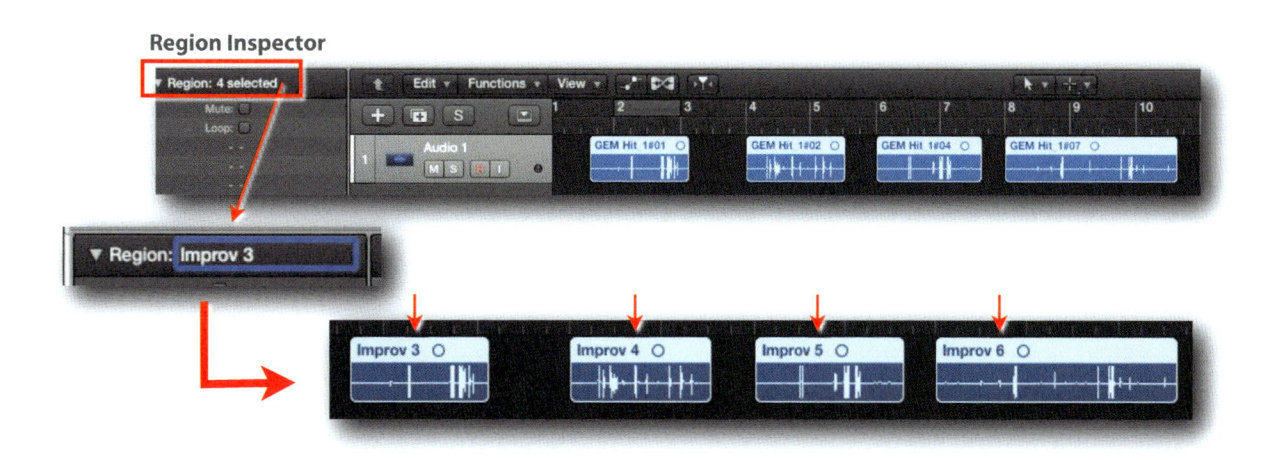

4 - Did you Know?

Copy Entire Track including Region and Automation

➤ Review

Logic has a very useful command "New Track With Duplicate Settings" that creates a new Track and assigns it to a new Channel Strip with the same set of Plugins and identical settings (Fader position, Pan position, Sends, Flex Modes, etc.) as the currently selected Track.

There are three ways to use that command:
- Menu Command *Track* ➤ *Other* ➤ *New Track With Duplicate Settings*.
- Key Command (*New Track With Duplicate Settings*) **cmd+D**.
- **Click** on the special Plus Button on top of the Tracks List ❶.

However, the command doesn't copy any Regions or Automation data from the selected Track. If you need that too, then you have to copy that manually in a separate step. But, there is a way to duplicate a Track with "everything on it".

➤ Attention

There are two drag procedures for a Track:

Move a Track

Drag the Track Header of any Track (even multiple selected Tracks), to move that Track up or down on the Tracks List to reposition it (the Mixer follows the Track order).

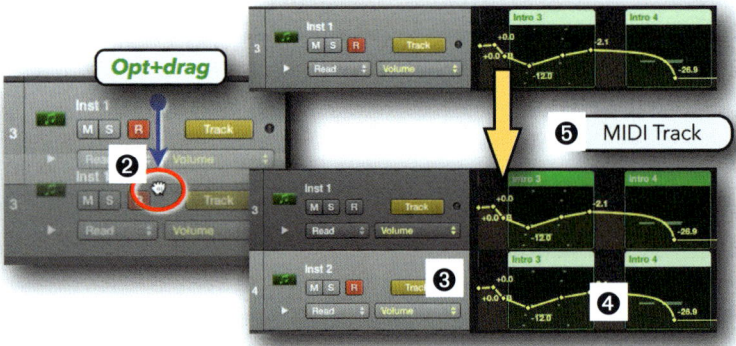

Copy a Track

Opt+drag also moves that Track ❷ (only one at a time) to a new position, but this time it makes a duplicate of the original Track, a complete duplicate:
- A new Track is created ❸, assigned to a new Channel Strip.
- The Channel Strip includes the same Plugins with identical settings of the Plugin controls and any other control on the Channel Strip (Fader, Pan, Sends, etc.).
- All the Automation data is copied over ❹.
- All the Regions are copied over. But here is an important difference:
  - **MIDI Regions** ❺: The copied MIDI Regions are independent copies of the original MIDI Regions.
  - **Audio Regions** ❻: The copied Audio Regions are not independent Audio Regions, they are clones. That means, changing the Region borders or the Anchor Point of the original Region will change that too on those copied Regions. To convert cloned Regions to independent Regions, use the command "Convert to New Audio Region", available in the *Edit* ➤ *Convert* menu or as a Key Command (*Convert Regions to New Regions*) **opt+cmd+R**.

Global Tracks Protect Button

➡ Review

One of the Track Header Components (the controls visible on the Track Header) is the Track Protect Button. It is hidden by default and must be enabled first.

- **Ctr+click** on the Track Header and select from the **Shortcut Menu ➤ Track Header Components ➤ Show/Hide Track Protect**.

- Open the Track Header Configuration Popover to enable the checkbox ❶:
  - **Ctr+click** on the Track Header and select from the **Shortcut Menu ➤ Track Header Components ➤ Configure Track Header...** .
  - Menu Command **Track ➤ Configure Track Header...** .
  - Key Command (*Configure Track Header*) **ctr+T**.

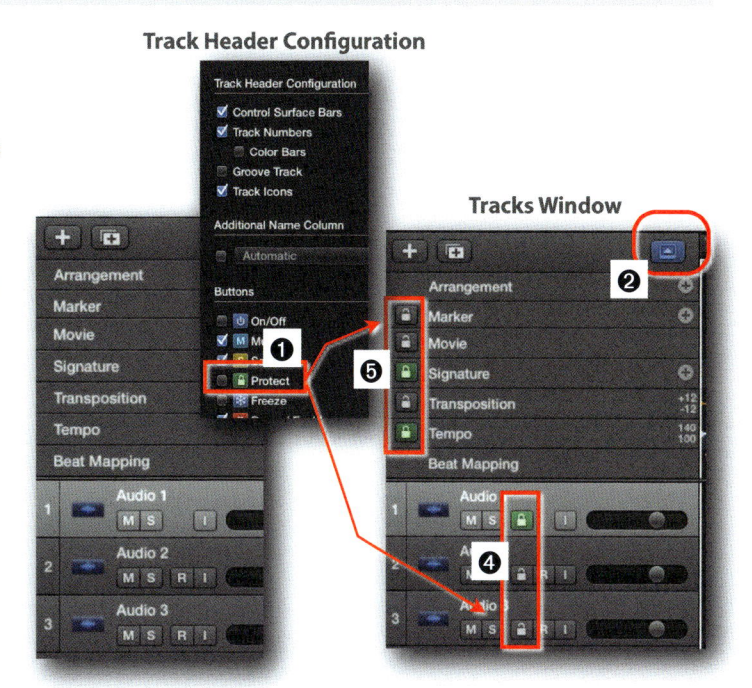

But in addition to protecting each Track, you can also protect the various Global Tracks from accidental edits.

➡ Attention

The Global Tracks can be displayed 🔲 in the Tracks Window ❷, but also in the various Editor Windows ❸. The procedure to show/hide it is slightly different.

💡 Tracks Window

The command to show/hide the Track Protect Button on the Track Header toggles it on all the Tracks ❹ and the Global Tracks ❺, except the Arrangement Track and Beat Mapping Track.

💡 MIDI Editors

There is a different command to make the Track Protect Button visible on the Global Tracks in the MIDI Editors ❻. Select the Local Menu **View ➤ Global Track Protect Button** ❼.

Attention There are a few things you have to keep in mind:
- ▶ The visibility of the Track Protect Button doesn't affect the functionality. Protect can be active even if the button is hidden.
- ▶ Although the show/hide status on the Tracks Window ❺ and the Editor Windows ❻ are independent, the actual effect, "protected or not protected", is linked.
- ▶ You can set the show/hide status independently on all MIDI Editors (Piano Roll, Score, Step Editor).
- ▶ If you try to edit a protected Global Track or regular Track, you will be prompted with an error message ❽. However, you can still edit a protected Global Track in its List Window.

Tear off Floating Window Panes

➡ **Review**

I cover a lot of topics about window management, because this is a major workflow consideration in Logic and also other professional apps. One special feature in Logic is the ability to "tear off" an area of a window, a so-called window pane, and make it a separate standalone window. There are a few details to be aware of.

➡ **Attention**

There are two procedures when it comes to tearing off windows:

- 💀 **Window Pane or Standalone Window**

With this procedure, you tear off a section to display that area as a standalone window instead of a window pane.

- ▸ In the Main Inspector, you can tear off the Movie Area ❶, Region Inspector ❷, and Group Inspector ❸.
- ▸ You *click-hold* on the Header Label ❹ and *drag* it away from the window ❺. Once you release the mouse, the window in the Main Inspector is removed ❻.
- ▸ The window will reappear in the Main Inspector, once you close the standalone window.
- ▸ Please note that you can open Logic's Main Window multiple times (*cmd+1*). Tearing off, for example, the Region Inspector as a new window only affects that specific window. The other Main Window(s) still displays the Region Inspector as part of their Main Inspector. The exception is the Movie Area. It is displayed only once, in the Main Inspector of the last Active Main Window.

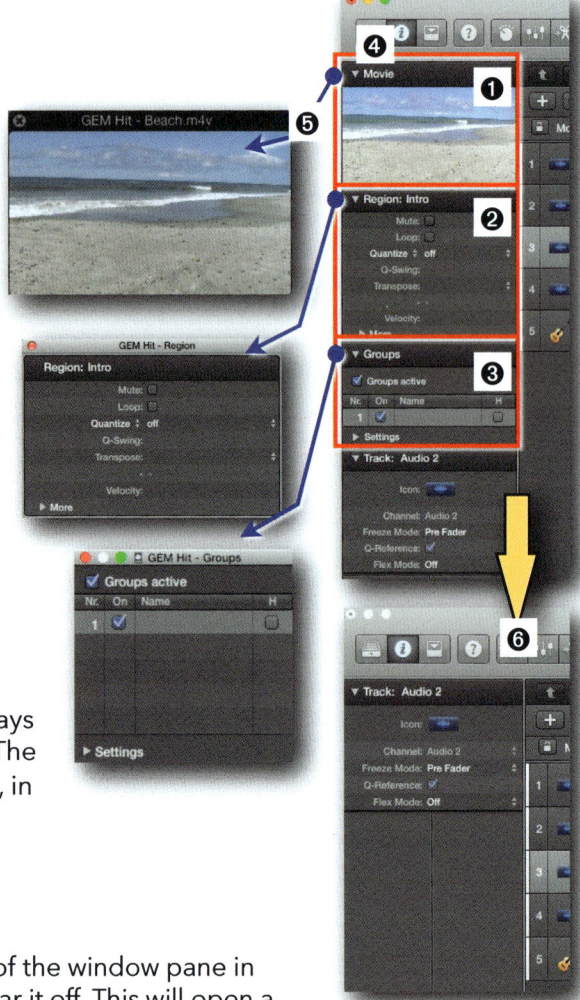

- 💀 **Window Pane and Standalone Window**

With this procedure, you *click-hold* on the blue tab ❼ on top of the window pane in Logic's Main Window and *drag* it away from the window to tear it off. This will open a new standalone window without removing the original window pane from Logic's Main Window. This works with pretty much all the windows that can appear as window panes inside Logic's Main Window and as separate standalone windows:

- ▸ **Editors**: Piano Roll, Score, Step Editor, Audio File Editor (not the Audio Track Editor).
- ▸ **Lists**: Event List, Marker List, Tempo List, Signature List.
- ▸ **Browser**: Project Audio Browser.
- ▸ **Exceptions**: Smart Controls and Mixer can be opened as standalone windows, but they don't have a button to be torn off from their window pane in Logic's Main Window.

Remove the Group Inspector (kind of)

➡ **Review**

The Channel Strip Group feature has one annoying side effect. Once you assign the first group ❶ to a Channel Strip in your Project, it will add the *Group Inspector* ❷ to the Main Inspector in Logic's Main Window. This is fine, but if you decide that you don't need Groups anymore and remove them from your Channel Strips, then the Group Inspector still stays in the Main Inspector and you cannot get rid of it anymore.

At least there is one workaround, not perfect, but better than nothing.

➡ **Attention**

Here are the steps:

- ☑ One cool feature of the Group Inspector, that I just described in the previous section, is that you can tear it off from the Main Inspector. Just *drag* its Header away from the Main Inspector ❸ and it will become a Floating Window ❹ removed from the Main Inspector (same behavior as the Region Inspector and the Movie Area in the Main Inspector).
- ☑ Now, move the Header ❺ of the Floating Window all the way to the bottom of the computer screen ❻, so only the Header is visible.
- ☑ At least, what you have achieved is that the Group Inspector is removed from the Main Inspector and now uses as little as possible screen real estate. It is almost out of the way (out of sight).

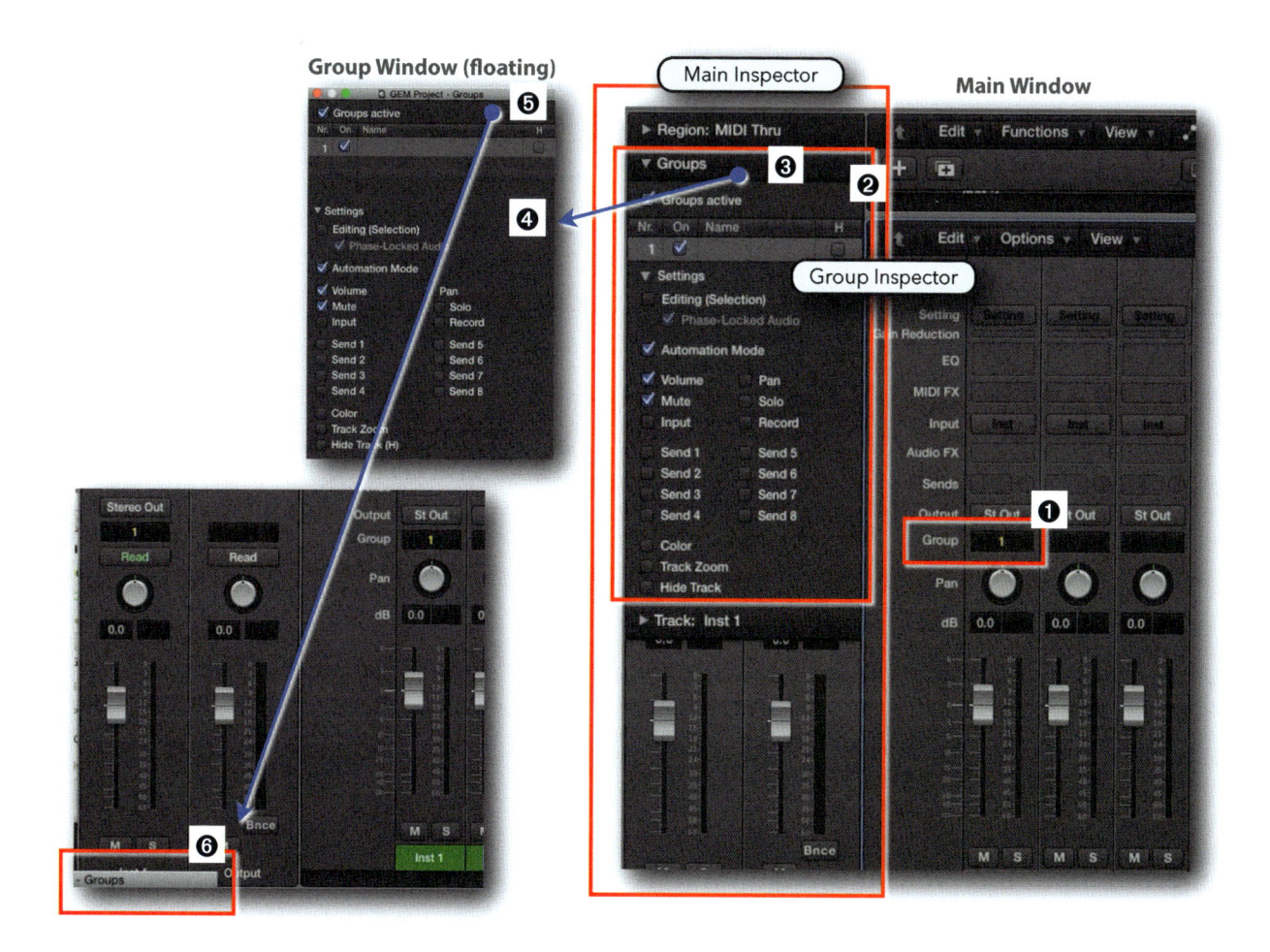

4 - Did you Know?

77

Mixer

Change Plugins and Aux Sends on Multiple Channel Strips at Once

➡ *Review*

Logic has multiple ways to group Channel Strips:
- ▸ *Channel Strip Groups*: This is the main grouping feature with its own Group Slot on the Channel Strip and its separate Group Settings window.
- ▸ *Aux Groups*: This is the old fashion way to route the audio signals of multiple Channel Strips to the same Aux Channel Strip.
- ▸ *VCA Groups*: This is the new feature in LPX, introduced in v10.1.
- ▸ *Ad-hoc Groups*: This is the most overlooked grouping feature that provides some quick and easy (and unique) grouping functionality.

➡ *Attention*

Here are some examples on how to use an Ad-hoc Group:

🔘 Create a Group

First, you create a group of Channel Strips by simply selecting those Channel Strips.
- *Click* on the first Channel Strip (on its background, not on a control), and then *sh+click* on a Channel Strip to the left or right. This will select all Channel Strips between them.
- The same can be accomplished by *shift+dragging* across multiple Channel Strips to select them all.
- *Cmd+click* on a series of non-contiguous Channel Strips to select only those.
- Use the *sh+click* and *cmd+click* to also de-select already selected Channel Strips.
- Any action you apply to the entire Group can be reverted with the undo command.

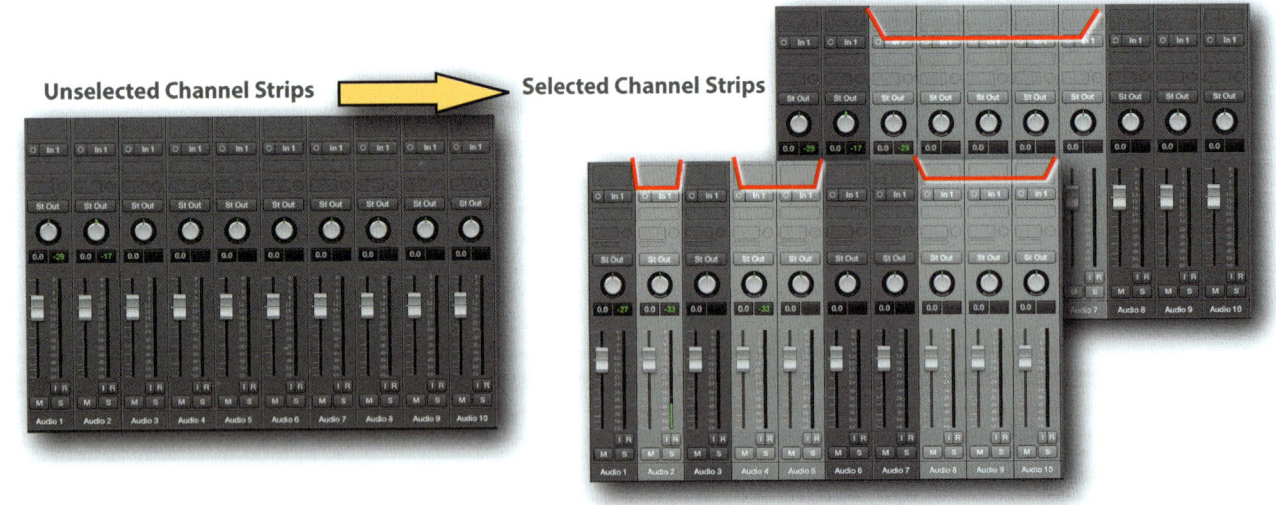

Unselected Channel Strips → **Selected Channel Strips**

🔘 Adjust Controls and Buttons

Once you've selected a group of Channel Strips, you can adjust any control (Fader, Pan, Sends), and the same control of all the selected Channel Strips will change simultaneously. Only the change will be applied as an offset, keeping their relative position to each other. You also can use any buttons (Mute, Solo, Rec Enable) on a Channel Strip to toggle that button on all selected Channel Strips. In this case, they all follow the same status of the button.

💡 Add Plugins

The power of the ad-hoc Group lies in this functionality that is not possible with any of the other grouping techniques. When you add (or remove) a Plugin to a Plugin Slot on one Channel Strip, then that Plugin is loaded to the same Plugin Slot on all the other selected Channel Strips. This really comes in handy when you want to quickly add an EQ or a compressor to a bunch of Channel Strips (drums, backing vocals, etc).

A few things to keep in mind:
- ▶ Plugins will only be added to an empty Slot and do not replace any existing Plugins.
- ▶ Using the "No Plug-in" option from the Plugin Menu removes the Plugin on that Slot for all the selected Channel Strips.
- ▶ The Power Button on the Plugin Button (that appears when you move the mouse over the button) has no affect on the Group and only toggles that individual Channel Strip.

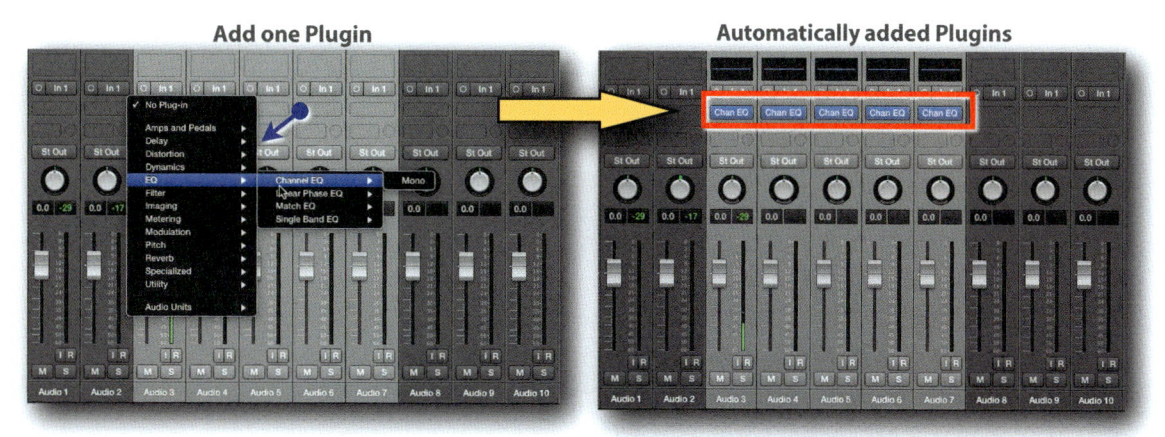

💡 Add Aux Sends

The same technique can be used for adding Aux Sends to a group of Channel Strips with one action.

A few things to keep in mind:
- ▶ Be careful, unlike with the Plugin Slots, the selected Send Slot will overwrite any existing Send Slot selection on the other selected Channel Strips.
- ▶ Using the "*No Send*" option from the Send Menu removes the Aux Send on that Slot for all the selected Channel Strips.
- ▶ The Power Button on the Send Button (that appears when you move the mouse over the button) has no affect on the Group and only toggles that individual Channel Strip.

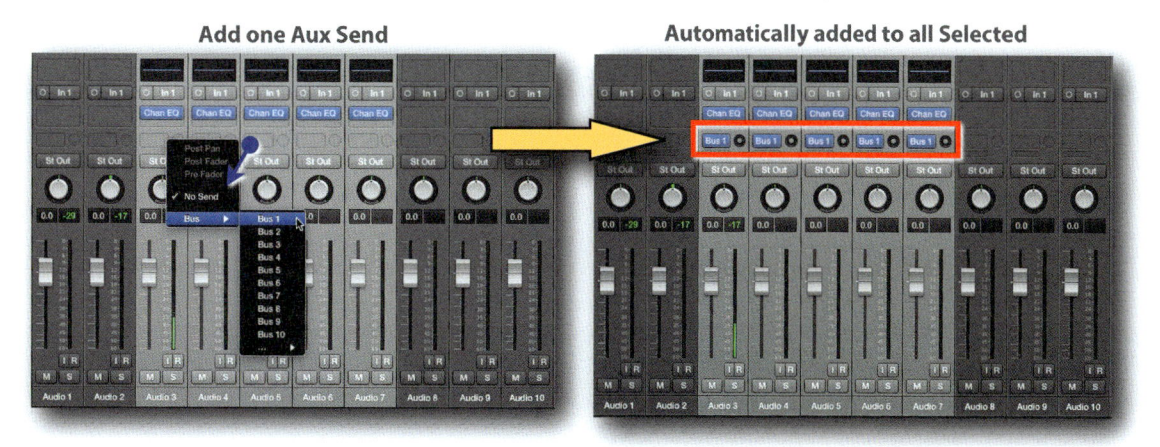

💡 Add the same Group assignment

You can even add Channel Strip Groups to all selected Channel Strips at once.

Add EQ or Compressor with One Click

4 - Did you Know?

➡ **Review**

The Channel EQ and the Compressor are perhaps the most used Plugins on your Channel Strips. To add them to a Channel Strip is as simple as *clicking* on the Plugin Button ❶ and selecting them from the Plugin Menu ❷. However, there are faster ways to do that.

➡ **Attention**

There are two Channel Strip Components that are visible by default. You can toggle them in the Channel Strip Component Window ❸ (in the popup menu or in the separate Popover window):

- **Gain Reduction Meter** ❹: When the Compressor Plugin (or the Limiter or Adaptive Limiter) is loaded on the Channel Strip, then this purple meter displays the amount of gain reduction.
- **EQ Thumbnail** ❺: This area displays the frequency curve of the Channel EQ Plugin. If you've automated your EQ parameters, then the displayed curve will even update in real time.

🔘 **Click Functionality**

- Plugin not loaded yet ❻: If the Plugin is not loaded yet, then *click* on the area to load the Compressor or Channel EQ to the Channel Strip.
- Plugin already loaded ❼: Once the Plugin is loaded, then a single *click* on the Gain Reduction Meter or the EQ Thumbnail will toggle the Plugin Window (open-close).
- You can also click on the EQ Button ❽ or the Plus Button ➕ ❾ in the Smart Controls Window to add the Channel EQ Plugin to that Channel Strip.

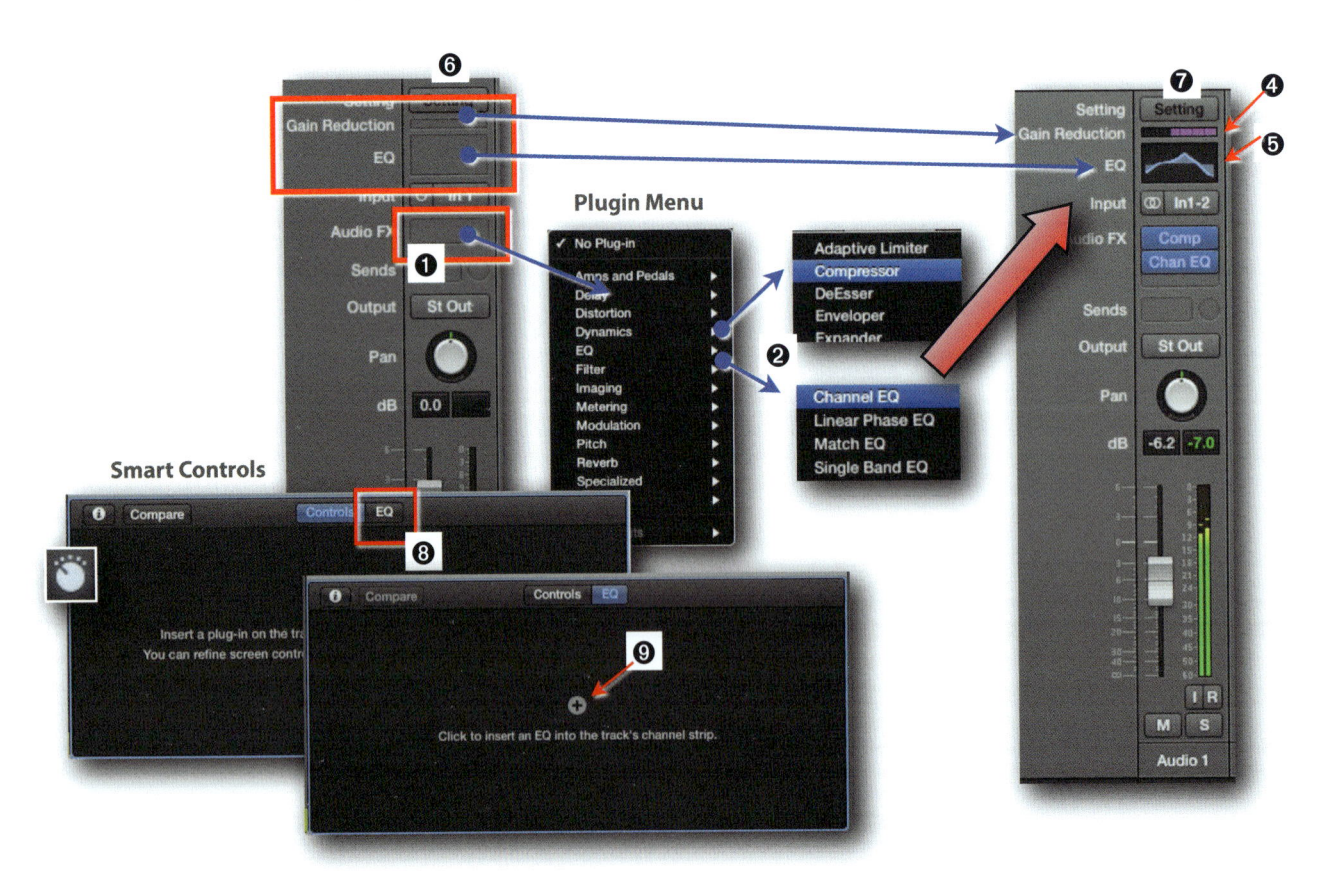

80   4 - Did you Know?

Toggle Plugin and Sends on/off

➡ Review

A big part of the mixing process of a Project is dealing with the Plugins and Sends, not only to look for the right Plugins and load them onto the Channel Strip, but also turning already loaded Plugins or Sends on and off are important steps. Make sure you know the available commands.

➡ Attention

There are four ways to toggle a Plugin or a Send on and off:

- ▶ Move the mouse over the Plugin Button or Sends Button to reveal its Power Button ⏻ ❶. *Click* on it to toggle it on or off.
- ▶ *Opt+clicking* on a Plugin Button ❷ or Sends Button was the old method before the Power Button was available. This command still works.
- ▶ *Drag* up or down a row of Plugins ❸ to turn them all (or the ones you drag over) on or off in one swipe (regardless of their previous state). Unfortunately, there still is no single "All Plugins on/off" button for a Channel Strip, besides some elaborate Environment setups.
- ▶ Of course, you can toggle the Power Button directly on the Plugin Window ❹.

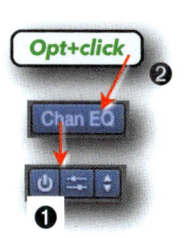

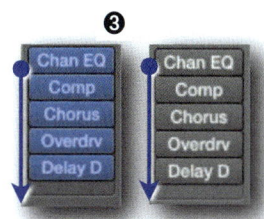

Reset Channel Strip

➡ Review

Loading and unloading Plugins on a Channel Strip during a mix is getting to a point where you sometimes might want to start from scratch.. For that, there is a special Key Command "Reset Channel Strip".

➡ Attention

The Command "Reset Channel Strip" ❺ is only available as a Key Command that is not assigned by default. Select a Channel Strip or multiple Channels Strips to reset them to their default settings ❻:

- ☑ No Plugins and Sends
- ☑ No Groups and VCA Assignment
- ☑ Fader at 0dB and Pan at center
- ☑ Default Track Icon
- ☑ Output set to Stereo Out
- ☑ Not affected: Input, Track Name, Track Notes

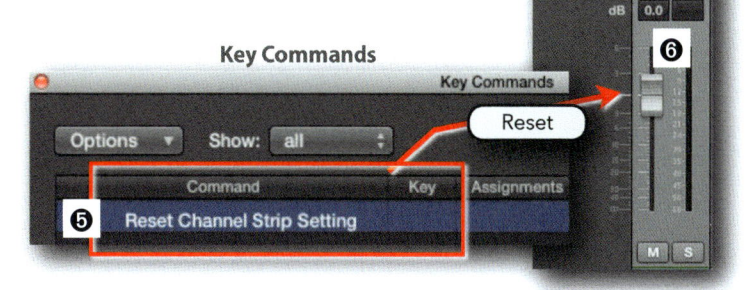

Numerical Entry of Onscreen Controls (with Decimal Points)

➡ Review

You change the value of any onscreen control (Fader, Slider, Knob) by moving it with the mouse or your external control surface. Another option is to enter a specific value numerically.

➡ Attention

To set the value for an onscreen control numerically, you *double-click* on the control which opens a text entry field that has key focus, indicated by the blue frame around it. Just type in the value and hit enter.

There are a few things to be aware of:
- All the controls on the Channel Strip (Volume ❶, Pan ❷, Sends ❸), and also on the Track Header (Volume ❹, Pan/Sends ❺) can be entered numerically.
- Only a few Plugins allow the entry of numerical values (i.e., Channel EQ ❻, Compressor ❼).
- Onscreen controls on the Smart Controls can't be entered numerically.
- Values can be entered with a decimal (13.2dB), which makes it much quicker to set a control to a precise value ❶.
- On the Channel Strip Fader, you can click on the Fader knob or the Volume Display above ❽.
- Please note that the Volume Display shows the "minus" sign only for single digits but not for double digits. A Fader position of "-13.0dB" ❾ will be displayed as "13.0".

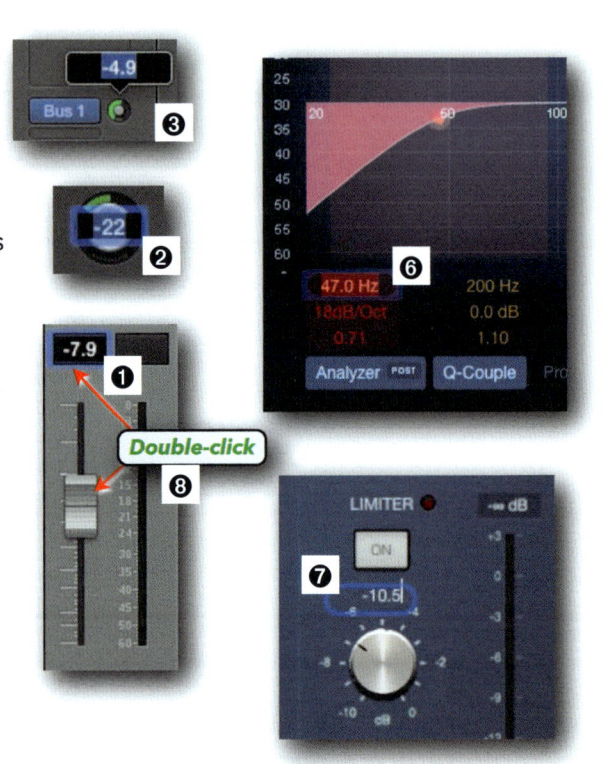

Here is a tip:

You can use the numerical entry to record an Automation Curve with a sudden value change. Let's say the value of the Volume Fader is 0dB and you want to drop it to -10dB at bar 5:
- ☑ Set Automation to Latch Mode
- ☑ Start playback before bar 5
- ☑ Double click on the Fader and type in -10
- ☑ At bar 5, hit return and the -10dB value will be written, including a Control Point for the previous value (0dB) a few Ticks before to create that sudden level drop ❿.

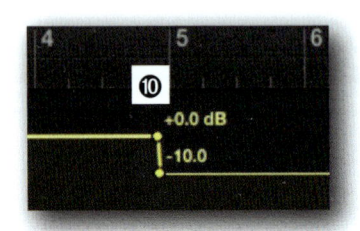

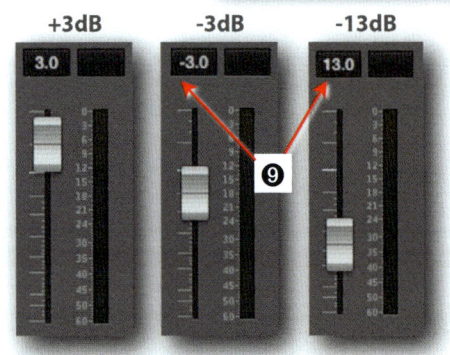

Signal Flow Inspector Channel Strip

➡ Review

The two Channel Strips under the Main Inspector in Logic's Main Window are the "Inspector Channel Strips". They have special functionalities that you definitely have to be aware of to make full use of it and speed up your workflow in Logic.

➡ Attention

🎯 Left Channel Strip ❶

The left Channel Strip always displays the Channel Strip assigned to the Track that is currently selected in the Tracks List. If multiple Tracks are selected, then it displays the Track that was first selected in a group of Tracks. See the topic "Indication for the first of multiple Selected Tracks" in this book.

🎯 Right Channel Strip ❷

The right Channel Strip is the so-called Signal Flow Channel Strip. It displays one of the Channel Strips that the Channel Strip on the left is routing its audio signal to. Which one depends on the following conditions:

- **Aux Channel Strip ❸**: *Clicking* on an Aux Send button ❹ on the left Channel Strip will display, on the right, the Aux Channel Strip that receives the Bus ❺ this Aux Send is sending to. This lets you quickly make adjustments on the Aux returns.
- **Output Channel Strip ❻**: *Clicking* on the Output Button ❼ on the left Channel Strip will display, on the right, the Output Channel that the left Channel Strip is routed to.
- **Master Channel Strip ❽**: If the Output on the left Channel Strip is set to "No Output", then the right Channel Strip will display the Master Channel Strip.

A few things to pay attention to:

You can configure the Inspector Channel Strips independently from the Channel Strips in the Mixer Window. **Ctr+click** on the Channel Strip and select *Channel Strip Components* ➤ ❾.

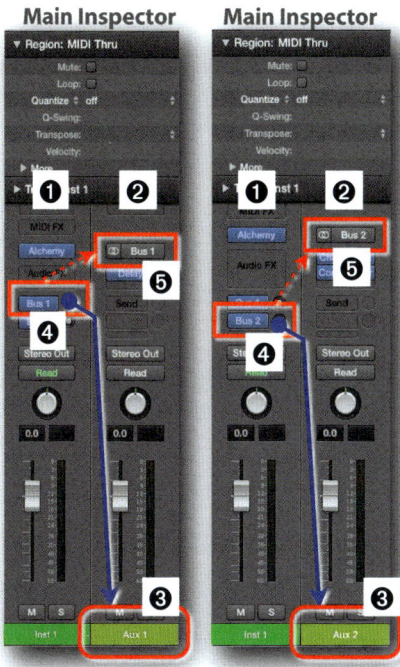

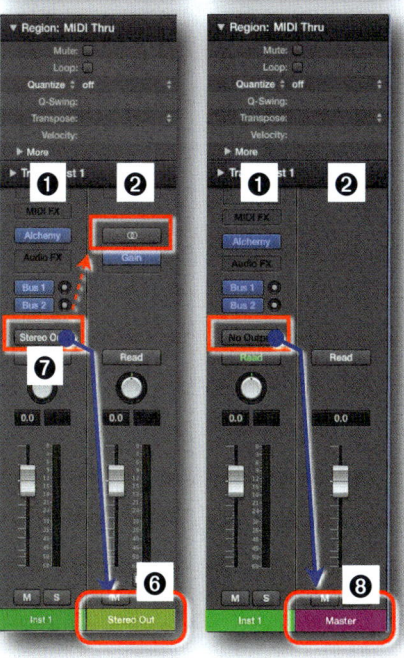

You can *click* to the left of any Plugin Button or the Setting Button on the left Channel Strip and right Channel Strip. This opens the Library Window (if it wasn't open) and displays the tiny blue triangle ❿ that indicates to which slot the Patch or Plugin Setting that is displayed in the Library will be loaded.

4 - Did you Know?

Show Aux Channel Strip of Used Bus Sends

➡ **Review**

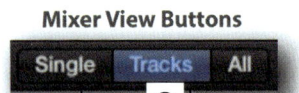

The Mixer View Buttons on top of the Mixer Window determine what Channel Strips are displayed in the Mixer Window and how. When "Tracks" ❶ is selected, then all the Channel Strips that are assigned to a Track in the Tracks Window are displayed, following the same order. In addition, any Channel Strip that is part of the signal flow (receives a signal from any Channel Strip in the Mixer) will also be displayed on the far right after the Channel Strips that are assigned to the last Track in the Tracks List. For example, Aux Tracks, Output Tracks, Master Track.

➡ **Attention**

If you have a Mixer Window with a lot of Channel Strips and/or using a small computer screen, then you constantly have to scroll the Mixer Window to get to a specific Channel Strip. One common task during mixing is that you use an Aux Send on a Channel Strip, and need to adjust the Aux Channel Strip the Aux Send is routed to, but, unfortunately, The Channel Strip is on the other end of the Mixer Window.

There are three ways to deal with that problem:

🔸 **Inspector Channel Strip**

This is the quickest way, which I just described in the previous topic "Signal Flow Inspector Channel Strip".

🔸 **Jump to Routed Channel Strip**

In the Mixer Window, *double+click* on any Aux Send Button ❷ (or the Output Button) and the Mixer Window selects the Aux Channel Strip that uses that Bus and scrolls ❸ the Mixer Window to display that Channel Strip on the far right of the Window.

🔸 **Assign Track**

This is also a nice workaround that involves a few extra steps:

☑ Create a Track for the Aux Channel Strip by *ctr +clicking* on the Channel Strip and selecting "Create Track" (Key Command *ctr+T*).

☑ Now you can place that Track, which is assigned to the Aux Channel Strip, anywhere in the Tracks List, for example, next to the Channel Strip that sends its signal via the Aux Sends.

☑ If you don't want to see the Track for the Aux Channel Strip in the Tracks Window, you can hide it from the Tracks Window (Key Command *ctr +H*), but you have to uncheck the "Follow Hide" ❹ option in the Local View Menu of the Mixer, so hidden Tracks are not hidden in the Mixer Window too.

84   4 - Did you Know?

Channel Strip Solo is "Signal Flow Aware"

➡ Review

Clicking on the Solo Button on a Channel Strip (or the Track Header) toggles "Channel Strip Solo" (not to be confused with Region Solo!). Any Channel Strip that doesn't have Solo enabled will be muted. That "forced-mute" status of a Channel Strip is indicated by a special blinking Mute Button [M] and not the regular solid Mute Button when you click on it [M].

However, when you use any routing to an Aux Channel Strip in your Project (via Aux Sends or the Output), then the Channel Strip Solo has some additional functionality that you should definitely be aware of.

➡ Attention

Logic's Channel Strip Solo feature is "Signal Flow Aware", which works as a forward and a reverse lookup.

Here is an example to show you what that means:

💀 Signal Flow - forward

Let's assume that you have a Channel Strip that uses its Aux Send to route its signal to an Aux Channel Strip where you add a delay effect. If you solo the Channel Strip, but want to hear it with the delay, then you have to solo the Aux Channel Strip too. Logic does that automatically, because it is aware of the signal flow (Channel Strip ➤ Bus ➤ Aux Channel Strip).

Here are three screenshots of a Mixer Window with three Instrument Channel Strips and three Aux Channel Strips. This is the Aux Send routing on the Instrument Channel Strip:

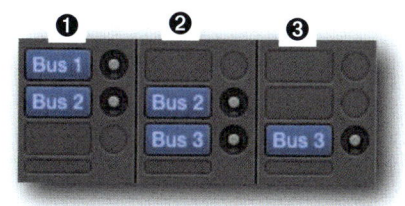

❶ Inst 1 is routed to Bus 1 and Bus 2.
❷ Inst 2 is routed to Bus 2 and Bus 3.
❸ Inst 3 is routed only to Bus 3.

Aux Channel Strip 1 is receiving Bus 1, Aux Channel Strip is receiving Bus 2, and Aux Channel Strip 3 is receiving Bus 3.

▸ In the first screenshot ❹, I soloed Inst 1. As you can see, Aux 1 and Aux 2 are not muted, because they receive signals from Channel Strip 1.

▸ In this screenshot ❺, I soloed Inst 2, and therefore, Aux 2 and Aux 3 are not muted.

▸ In this screenshot ❻, I soloed Inst 3, and therefore, only Aux 3 is not muted, because Inst 3 only uses Aux Send "Bus 3".

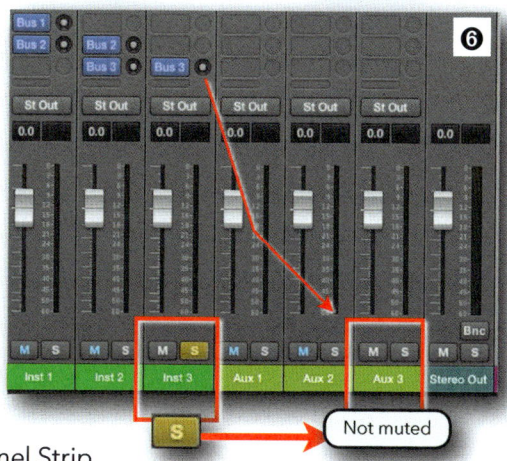

The Aux Channel Strips are also aware if you route to an Aux Channel Strip by selecting a Bus on the Output of a Channel Strip.

4 - Did you Know?

🎯 Signal flow - reverse

The same "Signal Flow Awareness" works in reverse.

When you solo an Aux Channel Strip, then Logic automatically solos any Channel Strip that routes its signal via an Aux Send to that Aux Channel Strip. Please note that the Aux Channel Strip that you put in Solo Mode has the yellow Solo Button [S] and the sending Channel Strips that are "forced-solo" have a special blinking Solo Button [S].

Here is the same Mixer setup showing what happens when you solo any of the Aux Channel Strips:

▶ In the first screenshot ❶, I soloed Aux Channel Strip 1. As you can see, Inst 1 is forced-solo too, because it is sending its signal to Aux 1 via its Aux Send.
▶ In this screenshot ❷, I soloed Aux Channel Strip 2. This time Inst 1 and Inst 2 are forced-solo because both Channel Strips are using Aux Sends to Bus 2.
▶ In this screenshot ❸, I soloed Aux Channel Strip 3. This time Inst 2 and Inst 3 are force-solo because both Channel Strips are using Aux Sends to Bus 3.

Aux Send vs. Output routing

Here is an example where Inst 1 is routing its Output signal ❹ to Aux 2 (via Bus 2) and Inst 2 is using its Aux Send ❺ to route to Aux 2 via Bus 2.

If you solo [S] Aux 2 ❼, then both feeding Channel Strips "stay un-muted", but in a different way.

- Inst 1 is just not muted ❽
- Inst 2 is using the forced-solo button [S] ❾

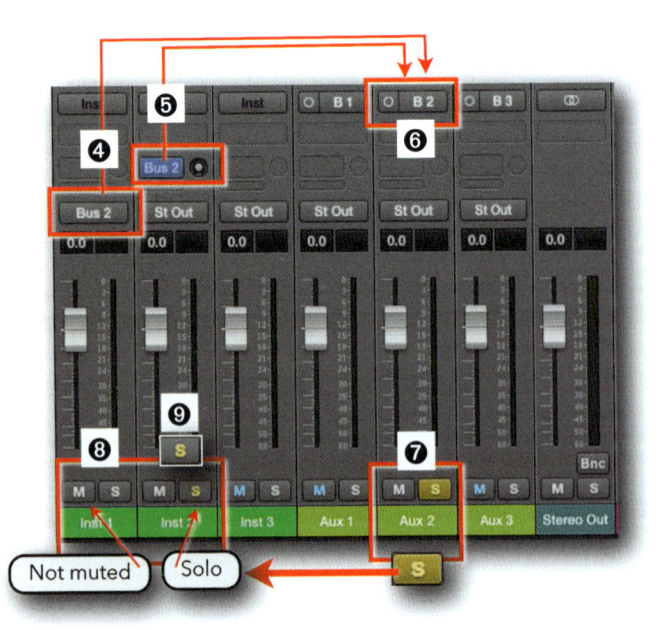

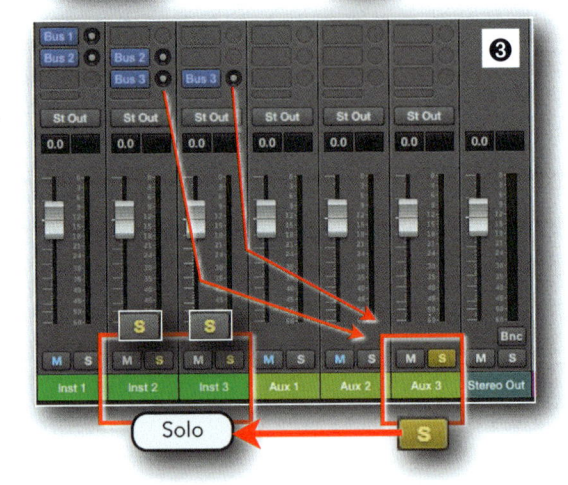

86   4 - Did you Know?

Workflow

Key Switcher

➡ Review

If you are using Orchestral Libraries, then you know the pain of using Key Switches to "trigger" different articulations of the same Instrument. For example, playing strings instruments in pizzicato, legato, or tremolo. There is an easy, but yet brilliant solution for that problem when using "**SkiSwitcher2**" by Peter Schwartz.

➡ Attention

SkiSwitcher2 has two components, a Macro that you copy to your Environment (super easy to do) and Plugin Settings for the MIDI FX Plugin "Scripter".

💀 The Concept

Usually, you play/record additional "dummy" notes, the so-called Key Switching Notes ❶, that act as a trigger to tell the Instrument to switch to a particular articulation ❷. For example, C0=legato, C#0=tremolo, D#0=pizzicato. With SkiSwitcher2 you still play the Key Switching Notes ❶, but they are not recorded in Logic anymore ❸!

Remember, each MIDI Note includes three properties: Pitch, Velocity, and MIDI Channel. The MIDI Channel is mostly set to the default ch1 and not really used much. SkiSwitcher2 utilizes that dormant MIDI Channel information in each MIDI Note as an embedded Key Switch indicator via a conversion table ❹ (i.e. C0=ch1, C#0=ch2, etc.).

When you play a keyswitch key ❶, it sets the MIDI Channel ❻ of the notes ❺ you play and record according to the conversion table ❹. Then, in real-time response to the MIDI Channel ❼ of the notes, the MIDI FX Scripter provides the patch with the actual keyswitch notes ❽ it needs to change articulations ❷. These keyswitch notes are sent internally in Logic directly to the Plugin and never appear in your MIDI recordings. The Instruments always play back the correct samples ❾.

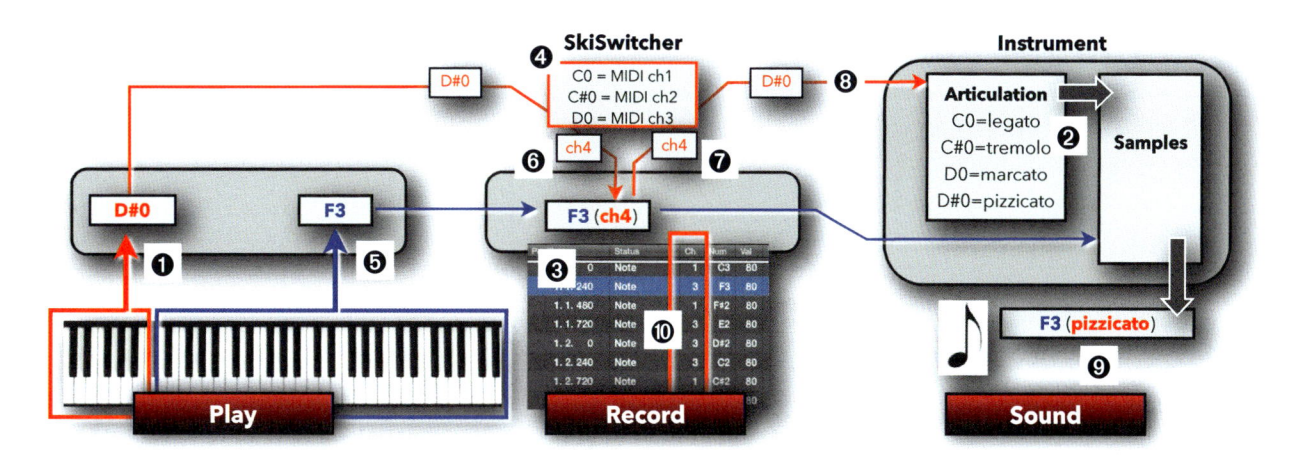

Advantages: There are no more dummy (Key Switch) notes in your Region (and Score) ... no "Chase" problems when playing back you Regions ... you can click on individual notes in your MIDI editor and they play with the proper articulation ... easily change the articulation of a note by changing its MIDI Channel ❿ ... you can even use the SkiSwitcher2 on multi-timbral Instruments ... and much, much more.
For more information, plus instructional videos, go to www.skiswitcher.com

5 - Be Aware!

Tracks Window

Confusing "New Track" Commands

➡ **Review**

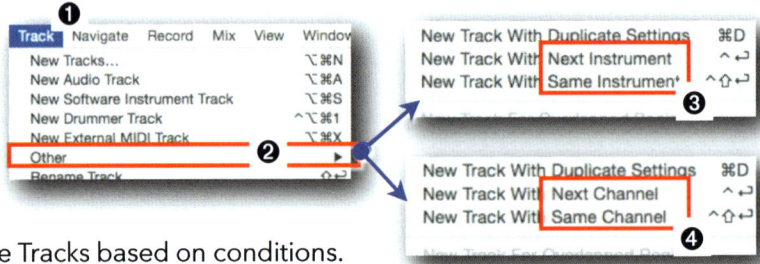

The *Tracks* Menu ❶ contains many commands to create the various Track Types, for example, Audio Track, Software Instrument Track, Drummer Track, and the External MIDI Track. The *Other* ❷ command opens a submenu with more options to create Tracks based on conditions. And that is where things can get confusing when you are trying to figure out what the meaning of those commands are.

First of all, depending on the currently selected Track, some wording changes to either *Instrument* ❸ or *Channel* ❹, and you should ask yourself, what is "Channel" referring to?

➡ **Attention**

To better understand the meaning of those New Track commands, you have to know about the underlying concept of Logic's Environment and the (slightly confusing) terminology Logic is using.

I explain all that in great detail in my book "Logic Pro X - How it Works". Here is a quick review about a few things you have to know regarding those New Track commands:

▸ Logic's Environment Window contains all the building blocks (the so-called **Environment Objects**) to create your virtual studio in your current Logic Project.

▸ One type of those Environment Objects are called the **Channel Strips**, which are grouped into seven **Channel Strip Types** (Audio, Instrument, Aux, Output, Input, Bus, VCA).

▸ Each Channel Strip Type has a limited number of available objects that are numbered through. These are the **Channel Strip Type No**, for example, Audio 1, Audio 2, Audio 3, ... Audio 256.

▸ The Track Inspector lists the Channel Strip Type and Number as the Parameter **Channel** ❺. The screenshot shows a Track assigned to an Audio Channel Strip (Audio 1) ❻ and an Instrument Channel Strip (Inst 1) ❼. Here, the Parameter "Channel" has nothing to do with a "MIDI Channel" !

▸ As you can see in the Software Instrument Track ❼, it has a separate Parameter labeled "MIDI Channel" ❽.

▸ Major Confusion Alert: If a Track is assigned to an External MIDI Instrument object ❾, then the Track Inspector also lists a Parameter labeled "Channel" ❿, but here, this is the MIDI Channel for that object and definitely should've been labeled "MIDI Channel".

Now let's look at the various commands while keeping that mis-labeled situation in mind:

💀 Series of Steps

A New Track command triggers the following steps:

▶ **Step 1**: Creates a new Track in your Project's Tracks Window.

▶ **Step 2**: Assigns an Environment Object to that Track.
- Audio Track is assigned to a Channel Strip object: "Audio 1" … "Audio 256"
- Software Instrument Track is assigned to a Channel Strip object : "Inst 1"…. "Inst 256"
- Drummer Track is also assigned to a Channel Strip object: "Inst 1"…. "Inst 256"
- External MIDI Instrument Track is assign to an Environment Object called "*Multi-Instrument*", which is a multi-timbral MIDI Instrument object.

▶ **Step 3** (optional): The Channel Strip can be configured (load Plugins, Sends, etc.).

💀 About Step 2: New or Existing Environment Object

There are two options when assigning an Environment Object to a Track:

▶ **New Object ❶**: All New Track commands, with the exception of one ❷, create a new Environment Object and assign it to that new Track. This is usually the next higher Channel Strip Type Number (External MIDI Instruments behave a little bit different). The currently selected Track only determines the position of the new Track in the Tracks Window, it will be placed below that Track.

▶ **Existing Object ❷**: Only one New Track command contains the word "Same" (*Same* Instrument or *Same* Channel). That command doesn't create a new Environment Object, it assigns the new Track to an existing Environment Object, the same one that is assigned to the currently selected Track.

💀 About Step 3: Channel Strip Setting

If you choose one of the New Track commands that assigns a new Environment Object ❶ to a new Track, then you could pre-configure its Channel Strip Settings (Plugins, Sends, etc.) upon creation of the Track.

▶ **Empty ❸** Channel Strip: These are the commands that create a Track with an empty Channel Strip (no Plugins, no Sends). However, the Input and Output routing on the Channel Strip (or the MIDI Object) is based on the current settings in the New Tracks Dialog:
- ❻ New Audio Track, New Instrument Track, New Drummer Track
- ❼ New Track with Next Instrument/Channel
- ❺ New Tracks...: You can choose in the New Tracks Dialog to create an *Empty Channel Strip*

▶ **Copy** settings from the currently selected Track: There is only one command that lets you copy the Channel Strip Settings from the currently selected Channel Strip to the newly created Channel Strip:
- ❹ New Track with Duplicate Settings (same as clicking the button)

▶ **Configure** the new Channel Strip with all the options available in the New Tracks Dialog. Please note that these settings are also used for newly created Tracks using the other commands ❻:
- ❺ New Track … (same as clicking the button)

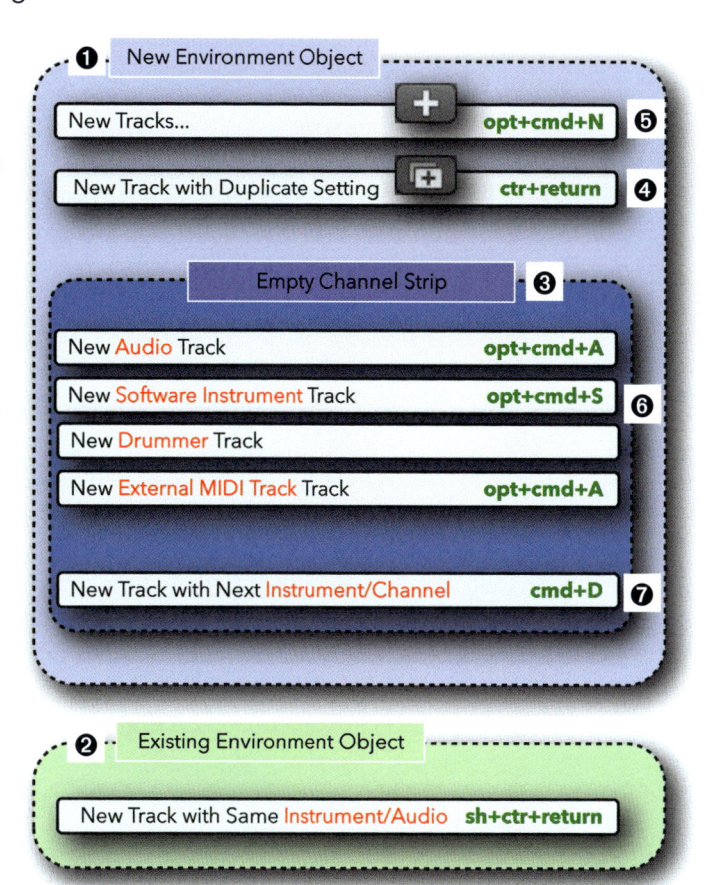

Which Channel Strip Types

Here is one little detail that can be easily overlooked:

▶ **Assign selected Environment Object**

By using any of the five commands in the Tracks Menu ❶, you select which Environment Object you want to assign to the new Track.

- <u>New Tracks</u>: The New Tracks Dialog lets you make the selection: Audio, Instrument, External MIDI Instrument.
- <u>New Audio Track</u>, <u>New Instrument Track</u>, <u>New Drummer Track</u>, <u>New External MIDI Track</u>: The selected command determines the type of Environment Object.

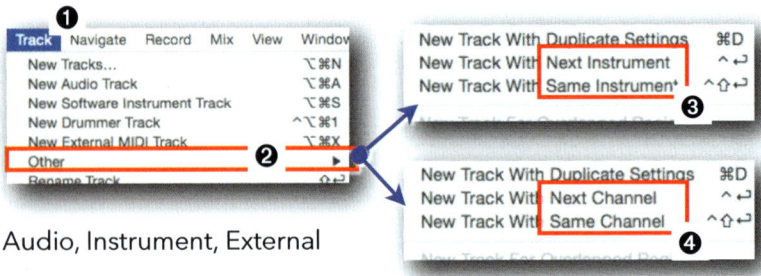

▶ **Assign Environment Object based on Track Selection**

When you use any of the five commands in the "Other" submenu ❷, then the Environment Object that will be assigned to the new Track will be the same type of Environment Object that is assigned to the currently selected Track. This enables you to assign any of the seven Channel Strip Objects to a new Track. For example, if the current Track is assigned to an Aux Channel Strip, then the newly created Track will also be assigned to an Aux Channel Strip. Of course, that new Aux Channel Strip will also show up on the Mixer Window.

The additional Channel Strip Types that are available are Aux, Bus, Input, Output (only in a Surround Project), and VCA (only in a Stereo Project).

Instrument vs Channel

Now let's finally go back to the original question about the term "Channel" and "Instrument" in the command:

▶ **Instrument**: If the currently selected Track is assigned to the Channel Strip Type "Instrument" ❺, then the menus display the command "Next Instruments" and "Same Instrument" ❸, referring to the Channel Strip Type "Instrument" ❻ listed under the Channel Parameter.

▶ **Channel (Channel Strip Type)**: All other Channel Strip Types ❼ (Audio, Aux, Bus, etc.) use the command "Next Channel" and "Same Channel" ❹. This refers to the **Channel** ❽ Parameter in the Track Inspector.

▶ **Channel (MIDI Channel)**: If the selected Track is assigned to the Environment Object "Multi-Instrument" ❾, then the menus also display the command "Next Channel" and "Same Channel" ❹. That also refers to the **Channel** ❿ Parameter in the Track Inspector, but keep in mind that, in this case, it is the actual MIDI Channel of that multi-timbral MIDI Instrument object.

Please Note

Keep an eye on the New Tracks Dialog. New Track commands that create a new empty Channel Strip still use the configuration for the Input and Output routing ⓫ that is currently set in the New Tracks Dialog (it remembers your last setting). This is also true for External MIDI Instruments.

90   5 - Be Aware!

Track Name vs. Channel Strip Name

➡ **Review**

In Logic Pro 9, the name you gave a Track was independent from the Channel Strip name that Track was assigned to. In Logic Pro X this behavior changed. Now, the Track Name ❶ is identical to the corresponding Channel Strip Name ❷. Changing a Track Name, changes its corresponding Channel Strip Name and vice versa ❸.

➡ **Attention**

If you hover the mouse cursor over the Track Name, a Tooltip ❹ pops up, indicating that it is the "Channel Strip Name".

💡 **Independent Track Name**

If you are one of the many Logic users who doesn't like this new behavior and wants to have independent Track and Channel Strip naming, then you can use the following workaround to "force" the name on the Track Header to be an independent "Track Name".

- ✓ As a default, I renamed the Track to "Vocals". Hovering the mouse over the name in the Track Header confirms with the Tooltip that this is the Channel Strip Name ❺.
- ✓ Now, Show the Automation and click the Automation Subtracks Disclosure Triangle ❻.
- ✓ When I *double-click* on the Track Name now, the entry field displays "*Track Name" ❼. This is the first hint that Logic changed its behavior.
- ✓ I type in the name I want for the Track Name, in this example, I use the same name "Vocals" ❽ and hit return.
- ✓ Now when I move the mouse over the Track Name again, the Tooltip says "Track Name" ❾ instead of "Channel Strip Name" ❺.
- ✓ Now, that particular Track stays in the mode and you can go ahead and rename it to any other name. It is always the Track Name (and yes, you can hide Automation if necessary ❿).
- ✓ You can rename the Channel Strip differently without affecting this Track Name.
- ✓ **Revert**: To revert back to the "Channel Strip Name only Mode", *double-click* on the Name, hit *delete*, and then *return*. Of course, you can return to the separate naming convention any time by repeating the trick with the Subtracks Disclosure Triangle.

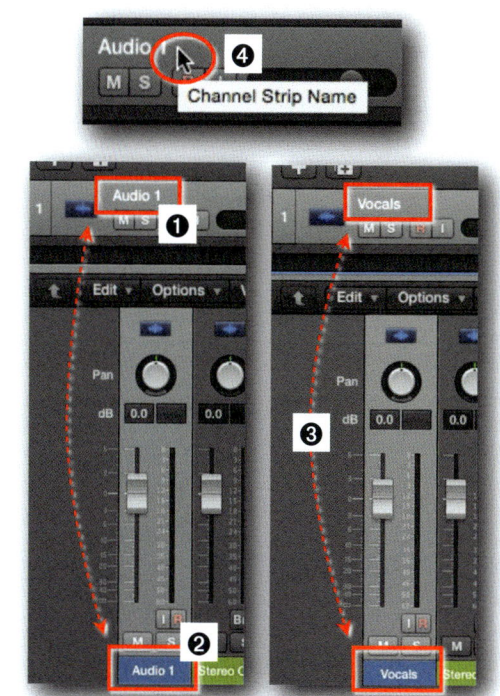

💡 **Option 2**

There is a second (not as elegant) workaround to switch to "Track Name" mode:

Select the Track you want to switch to independent Track Name behavior and use *sh+ctr+return* to create a new Track assigned to the same Channel Strip. When you *double-click* on the Name, it also shows the "*Track Name* ❼ to indicate that you can now enter an independent Track Name.

"Delete Automation" Commands Are Incomplete

➡ Review

Logic provides five commands ❶ that quickly let you delete specific Automation data. The name of the commands are very long to specify exactly what is deleted. Unfortunately, they are not long enough to explain exactly what data will and will not be deleted.

➡ Attention

Here are the five delete commands with the "full description":

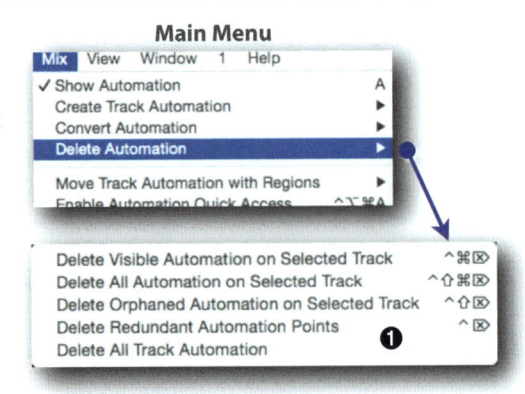

- **Delete Visible Automation on Selected Track**
  - *Delete Track Automation ❷ or Region Automation ❸ (whichever is visible) on the Main Track ❹ of the selected Track, not any visible Automation Subtracks ❺*

- **Delete All Automation on Selected Track**
  - *Delete all Track Automation or all Region Automation (whichever is visible) on the selected Track*

- **Delete Orphaned Automation on Selected Track**
  - *Delete all Orphaned ❻ Automation data of the Track Automation (not Region Automation!) of the selected Track*

- **Delete Redundant Automation Points**
  - *Delete Redundant ❼ Track Automation or Region Automation (whichever is visible) of the selected Track*

- **Delete All Track Automation**
  - *Delete All Track Automation in your Project (but none of the Region Automation)*

- **(Delete All Region Automation)**
  - *This command is only available as a Key Command (unassigned)*

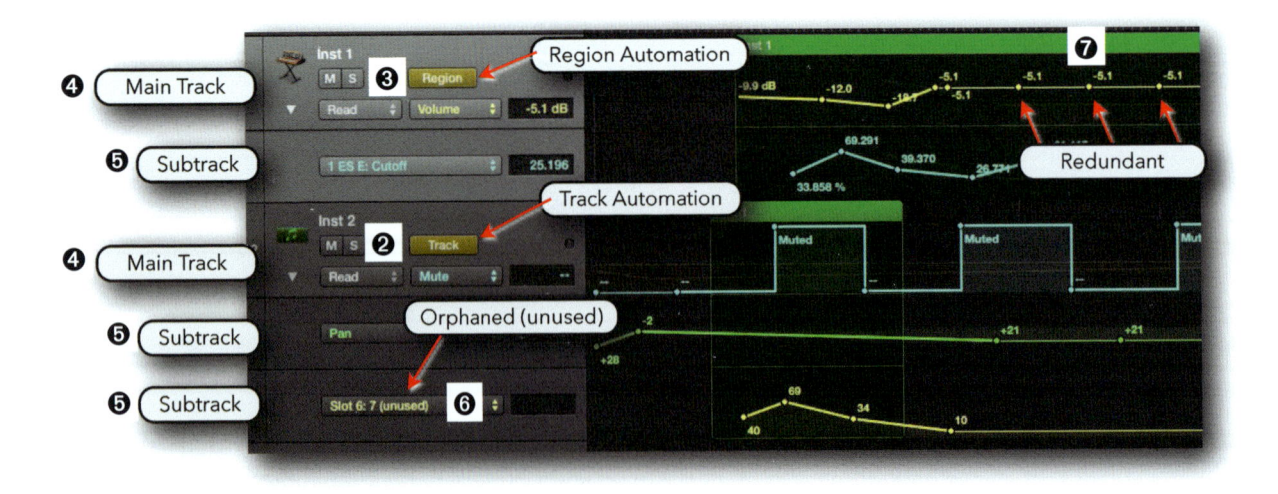

92   5 - Be Aware!

Editing

Project Type Sets the Unit for the Delay Parameter in the Region Inspector

➡ Review

The Region Inspector, as part of the Main Inspector in Logic's Main Window, contains a Delay Parameter ❶. You have to *click* on the Disclosure Triangle "*More*" ❷ to show it. This Parameter, which is available for all types of Regions (MIDI, Audio, Drummer, Folder), can apply a time offset to that Region. Although the term "Delay" implies that "something happens later", you can actually set the time offset to be a positive value (Region plays later), or a negative value (Region plays earlier).

Most likely, the time unit of the Delay is listed as "ticks", but it can also be milliseconds (ms). Plus, there are a few more little details. Please note that the following also applies to the Parameter "Q-Flam" and "Q-Range" of a MIDI Region:

➡ Attention

There are quite a few things you have to be aware of with this Delay Parameter:

🔘 Project Type sets the Delay unit to either ticks or milliseconds

There is an important and sometimes overlooked setting in the **Project Settings ➤ Global** called *Project Type* ❸. It switches the displayed time units on the Primary Ruler and the underlying grid.

☑ This is the default setting used for song-based Projects that rely on a bar/beats structure with a specific Tempo:
- The Primary Ruler displays Musical Time as bars and beats.
- The Delay Parameter is displayed in ticks ❹.
- The Delay popup menu also displays the equivalent of each tick value as time (ms) and note value (i,e, 1/16) ❺.

☐ This setting is for "free running" Projects that don't rely on a tempo and bar/beat structure (i.e. dialog recordings or live recordings):
- The Primary Ruler displays Absolute Time as minutes and seconds (SMPTE format).
- The Delay Parameter is displayed in ms (milliseconds) ❻.
- The Delay popup menu ❼ also displays the equivalent of each ms value as ticks (grid value) and note value (i,e, 1/16).

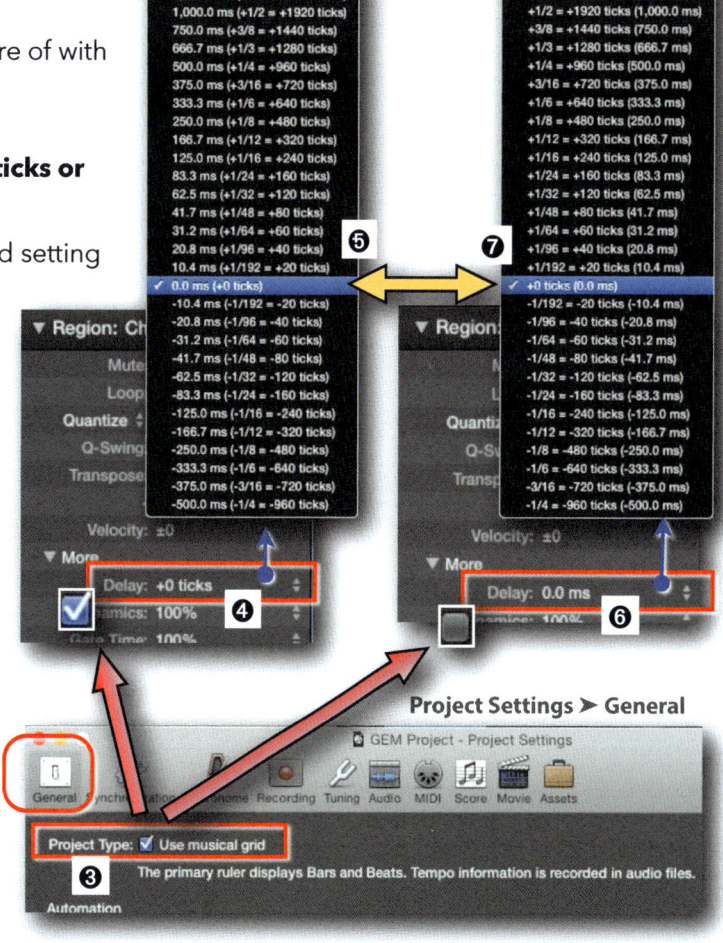

🔮 Tooltip

If you move your mouse over the Delay value in the Region Inspector, then a Tooltip will popup, displaying the delay value in all three units ❶.

🔮 Enter any value

You can set a delay value in three ways:
- 🔮 Select a value from the popup menu.
- 🔮 *Double-click* on the value, which opens an Entry Field, and type in the delay value.
- 🔮 *Drag* the value up or down to slide through the numbers.

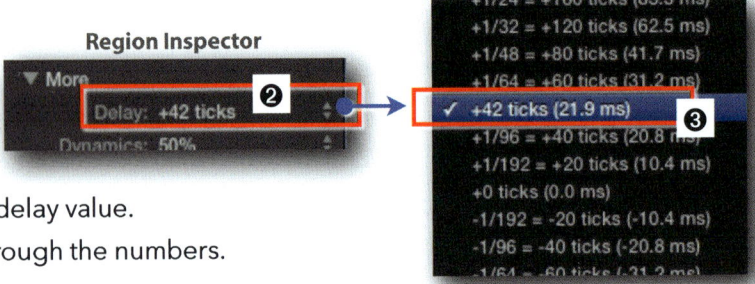

Here is one little detail: If you entered a value that is not listed on the popup menu ❷, then that value will be temporarily added. When you open the popup menu, you will see that the value is placed at the correct position of increasing and decreasing number values ❸.

🔮 MIDI Thru Parameter

A note of warning about the Delay value. The Region Inspector displaces the value(s) of the currently selected Region(s). If no Region is selected, then the values represent the so-called "*MIDI Thru*" Parameter indicated in the Region Header ❹. These are the Parameters that will be applied to any new Region you record or create. This is a handy feature when you want to automatically apply, for example, a 1/16th Quantization to every Region you record. However, if you set a Delay value while no Region is selected ❺, then that Delay value will also be applied to every new Region, which might not be what you wanted, wondering why all your new recorded Regions are out of sync.

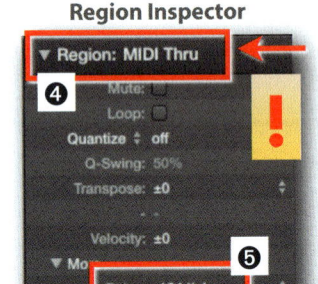

🔮 Minimum/Maximum Values

These are the minimum and maximum numbers that you can enter:
- 🔮 *Ticks*: -999 … +9,999
- 🔮 *Milliseconds*: The limits for the ms values are based on the limits for ticks. Therefore, the maximum and minimum value in milliseconds depends on the current Tempo (the slower the tempo, the longer the "duration" of a tick)

Two Separate Values for the Delay Parameter in the Track Inspector

➡ Review

As we have just seen, the little double arrow ❻ displayed next to the value of that Parameter indicates a popup menu that provides a list of values to choose from when you click on that arrow. For example, quantize values ❼ or MIDI Channels. Sometimes there is also a double arrow displayed right next to the Parameter itself ❽. This indicates that there is a popup menu that lets you further specify the Parameter. For example, the Quantize Parameter ❾ in the Region Inspector has a popup menu that lets you select either "Classic Quantize" or "Smart Quantize".

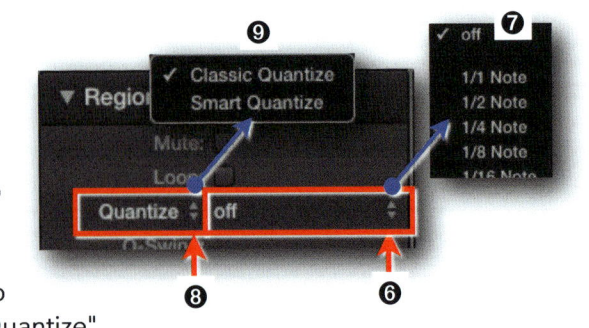

94   5 - Be Aware!

The Delay Parameter ❶ in the Track Inspector also has this double arrow, which provides a popup menu that lets you choose between two options ❷:

- **Delay in Ticks**
- **Delay in Milliseconds**

Let's have a closer look at that parameter, because the functionality might be quite different from what you expect.

➡ **Attention**

First, here are a few facts about that Delay Parameter ❶:

- ▸ The Delay Parameter is only available in the Track Inspector if the Track is assigned to a Software Instrument Channel Strip.
- ▸ The Delay Parameter adds a delay to the output of the Software Instrument (the sound generator).
- ▸ The value can be positive (signal sounds late) or negative (signal sound early).
- ▸ "*Delay in Ticks*" ❸ displays the delay value in Musical Time as Ticks. 960 Ticks equals one quarter note (the native time grid). Please note that the audible delay (Absolute Time) changes when you change the Tempo because the duration of a quarter note also changes due to Tempo changes.
- ▸ "*Delay in Milliseconds*" ❹ displays the value in Absolute Time as milliseconds (ms). Please note that now the audible delay is not affected when changing the Project Tempo.

Two independent Delay Values

We just saw with the Delay Parameter in the Region Inspector that the Delay value can be displayed in either ticks or ms. The misconception about this Delay value in the Track Inspector is that you might expect that it also just changes the units between ticks and ms. However, this is not the case. Ticks and ms represent two independent values. When you set the delay to 50ms and switch to ticks, then the Delay value doesn't display 50ms in ticks. Instead, it displays whatever value you have set there earlier, and therefore, the actual audible delay changes to that Delay value.

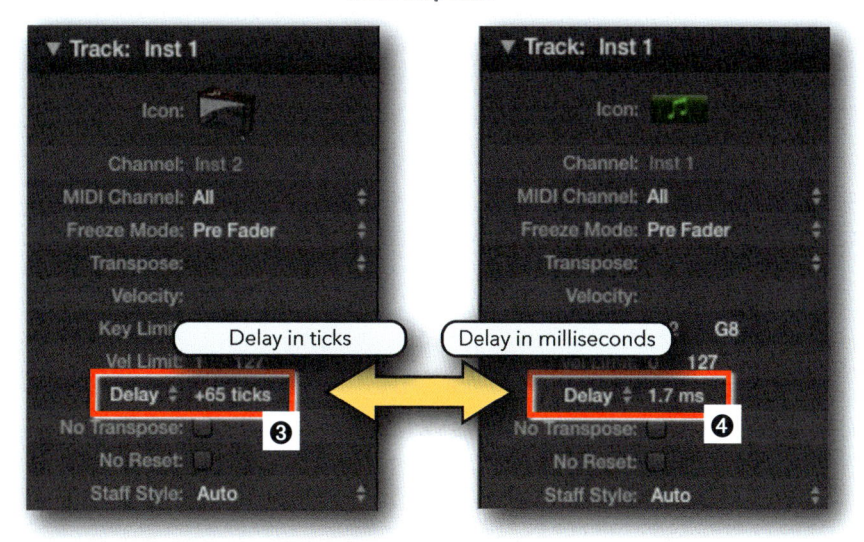

Default and Maximum Values

- *Default value*: The default value for a Track is 0 ticks and 0 ms.
- *Maximum Value*: The minimum/maximum values are ±99 ticks and ±500 ms.

5 - Be Aware!

Cut/Insert/Repeat Section Commands have Two Variations

➡ Review

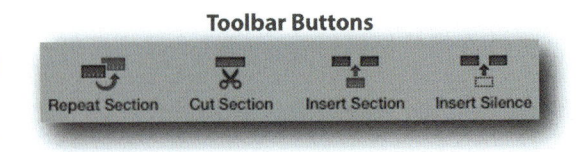

Usually, edits are performed by first selecting the Region(s) and then choosing the edit command. This tells Logic which Region is the "recipient" for the edit command. But Logic also provides editing commands where the "recipients" are defined by the range between the left and right Locator, which means, all the Regions inside the Cycle Range are the target.

These commands are grouped in the submenu "Cut/Insert Time" and have the word "Section" in it to indicate that you will edit an entire section in the Workspace, and therefore, affect the time structure of your Project. That means, this is potentially a dangerous command and should be used with special care. To make the command even more "dangerous", it has some hidden functionalities you should be aware of before using it.

➡ Attention

Here are the four commands accessible from different places:

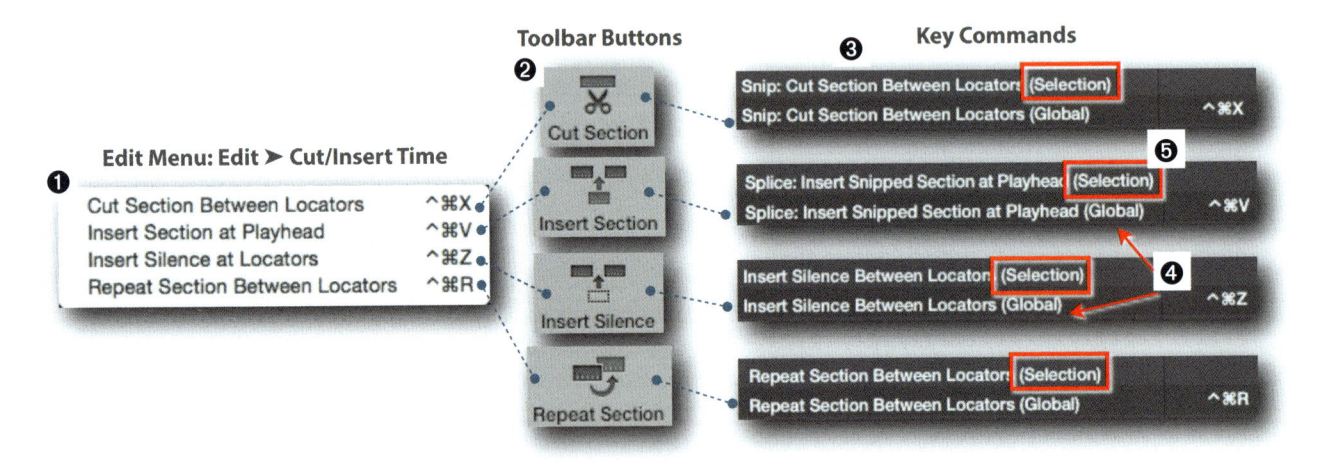

🔘 Affect all Regions including Global Tracks

When you use the Menu Command ❶, the Toolbar Button ❷, or the Key Command ❸ (the one with the word "*Global*") ❹, then all Regions between the Cycle Range are affected, no matter if they are selected or not.

🔘 Affect only selected Regions including Global Tracks

If you want to affect only the selected Regions inside the Cycle Range, then you can use the Key Command, the one with the word "*(Selection)*" ❺. These Key Commands have no key combination assigned by default. If you use those commands, an additional Dialog Window ❻ pops up where you select "*Move*" ❼ to also affect the Global Tracks.

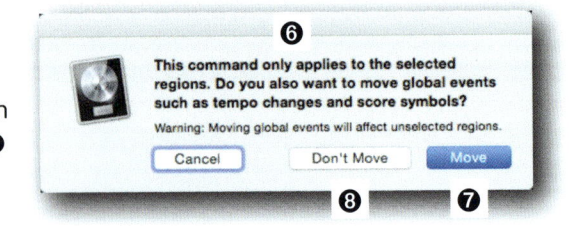

🔘 Affect only selected Regions excluding Global Tracks and Score Symbols

This is a variation of the previous procedure. Now you select "*Don't Move*" ❽ from the Dialog Window to leave the Global Track as they are and only affect the selected Regions inside the Cycle Range.

Dynamic Functionality of the "Show Editor" Command

➡ Review

The command "Show/Hide Editor" is available in three places:
- Main Menu: ***View ➤ Show/Hide Editor*** ❶
- Key Command *Show/Hide Editor* ***E*** ❷
- Editors Button ❸ in the Control Bar

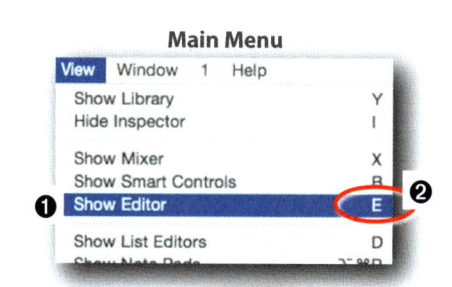

But first, a quick word about the terminology.
- ▶ **Window Pane**: This is a special area on a window. Logic's Main Window has many of those areas, and many of them can be toggled (shown/hidden) to use the space more efficiently while still staying on one single window.
- ▶ **Editor Window**: Some Window Panes display one dedicated content like the Library or Inspector on the left. Other Window Panes like the one on the right (Event List, Loop Browser, etc.) and at the bottom (Editor Window, Mixer, Smart Control), with additional tabs to switch between different views, can display a multitude of different windows. Let's look at just the Editor Window:

Logic has many different types of Editors for MIDI Regions and Audio Regions, or the Drummer Region, so the question is, which Editor will be displayed in that bottom Window Pane? The answer is not that simple, because this is one of those typical Logic features that has so many "if - then" conditions, that it is borderline confusing.

➡ Attention

In order to predict which Editor will be opened by the "*Show Editor*" command, try to remember the following order of rules:

Basic Rules

- ☑ If no Region is selected in the Project, then the Track Type determines what Editor Window opens up:
  - MIDI Track opens a MIDI Editor, Audio Track opens an Audio Editor, Drummer Track opens the Drummer Editor.
  - If multiple Tracks are selected, then the Track that was first clicked in that group determines the Editor.
- ☑ If a Region is selected, then the Region Type (Audio, MIDI, Drummer) determines what Editor Window opens up:
  - If multiple Regions are selected, then the Region that was first clicked in that group determines the Editor.
- ☑ The command even remembers the specific Editor Window. For example, the Piano Roll, Score, or Step Editor for the MIDI Editor, or the Audio Track or Audio File Editor in case of the Audio Editor.

Change the Editors of an open Window

Of course, once the Window Pane is open, displaying any of the Editors, then selecting any Region will change the specific Editor Window to match the Editor to the Region Type (MIDI, Audio, Drummer).

Close Editor Window

Of course, *Show/Hide Editor* is a toggle command so you also can use it to close the Window Pane, or you can ***click*** on the blue tab or the upper Divider Line of the Window Pane to close it.

Miscellaneous

Important Difference between Sheets and Popovers

➡ *Review*

Logic Pro X is an OSX application, and therefore, has to follow the Human Interface Guidelines that Apple dictates to guarantee a unique user experience across different apps on your Mac. It is not necessary that Logic users know those conventions and the proper terminology, but sometimes it is helpful to be aware of those, especially if they could negatively affect your work in Logic. Let's look at the Sheets and Popover:

🎯 Sheet

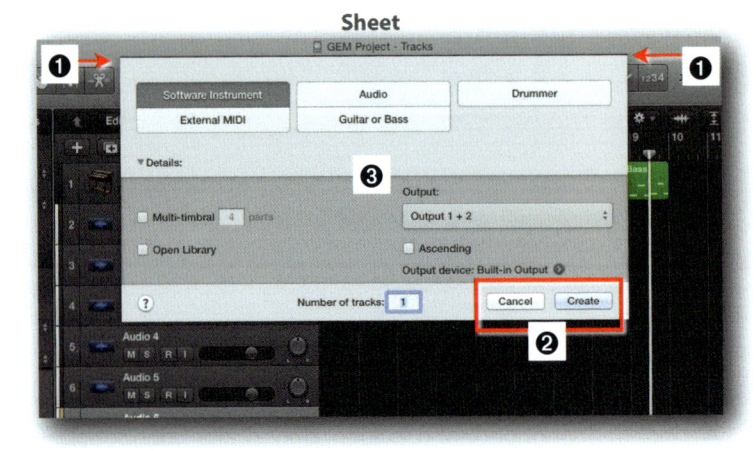

OSX provides a special type of Dialog Window called a "Sheet". These are windows that slide out from the top of the current window ❶ and prohibit you to interact with the current window until you close the Sheet again (a behavior called "Document Modal"). Those "closing buttons" ❷ can be "Save", "Create", "Done", or just "Cancel". Sheets are mainly used for Dialog Windows that let you configure components or let you make selections. Logic's *New Tracks Dialog* ❸ (*opt+cmd+N*) is one example. However, many others have changed in the LPX update v10.1 to a different type of Dialog Window, the so-called Popover Window.

🎯 Popovers

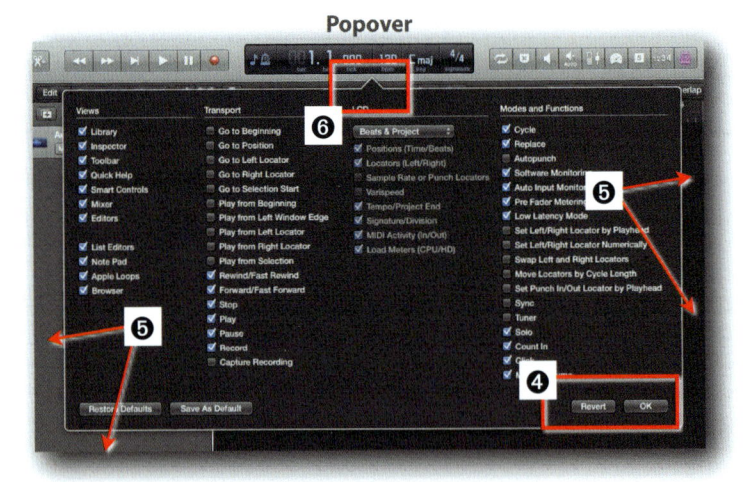

Popovers are also a type of Dialog Window in OSX that are similar to Sheets. The main difference is that they don't have to have a specific button to close the window ❹. In that case, you click on the background of the window behind, outside the Popover, to close the Popover window. BTW, the window has a pointer ❻ (the so-called Anchor) that points to the component it is affecting.

Popovers are mainly used to configure specific aspects of a component in an app. In Logic they are now used for:

- Control Bar Configuration
- Toolbar Configuration
- Track Header Configuration (*opt+T*)
- Channel Strip Configuration
- Global Tracks Configuration (*opt+G*)

➡ Attention

Popovers without a button to close them have a nasty side effect, a potential danger you have to be aware of. Even with a button to close, you can also click outside the Popover to close them.

But what could possibly go wrong there?

😎 Sheet vs. Popover

Here are two screenshots of the Track Header Configuration Window. The first one in the form of a Sheet ❶ (pre LPX v10.1) and second one in the form of a Popover ❷, the way it is now in LPX.

On the Sheet, you just clicked the "Done" ❸ button to close the window, but now, having a Popover, there is no button to close it ❹. You have to click outside it to close it. But before you do that, you have to know that the window behind is still active. That means, wherever you click, that position is an active click position (a functionality called "*click through*").

Here are two potentially dangerous scenarios:

- ▸ If the active window behind displays Automation, then clicking on that Automation Lane ❺ could create an Automation Control Point.
- ▸ If you have the Pencil Tool selected and move over the Track Header or the Control Bar, the cursor changes to the Pointer Tool and you can click there to bring up the command for opening the Popover to configure the Track Header or the Control Bar. While you move around the Popover to set the checkboxes, your cursor will still be the Pointer Tool. Now if you want to close the window you have to move the cursor outside. However, when you move to the right, over the Workspace, your cursor automatically changes back to the Pencil Tool and now clicking on the Workspace would close the Popover, but it would also create a new MIDI Region if you were to click on the Track Lane of a MIDI Track.

Input Focus - Consequences

➡ Review

There are a lot of things that Logic is doing in the background. Some of those things might require a lot of attention, which translates into used processing power. One reason to avoid that unnecessary activity is to minimize unwanted CPU usage, just to reduce heating up your computer (so the noisy fan doesn't kick in). A more important reason is to reserve CPU power for the task you want Logic to perform in the foreground, for example, recording, mixing, bouncing, etc. So be aware of what causes unwanted activities and know how to turn them off.

➡ Attention

One of the actions that puts Logic into "high alert" is the so-called Input Focus.

💡 Input Focus

Input Focus means that you tell Logic to watch out for (focus on) specific Tracks, especially what happens on their input. A Track has Input Focus when you do any of the following:

- ▶ **Select Input Monitoring** [I] ❶: This button tells Logic specifically to pay attention, to monitor that Track. That means, even if Logic is not playing and you think it is doing nothing, it is actually processing that signal on that Channel Strip, even in Stop Mode. Having Software Monitoring 🔊 enabled tells Logic to route that input signal through the Channel Strip, processing with all the Plugins that you have loaded up on that Channel Strip.

- ▶ **Select Record Enable** [R] ❷: This button has a similar effect as the Input Monitoring Button regarding the signal routing through the Channel Strip. In addition, when you just play back and are not in Record Mode, Logic is already recording in the background if you have "Allow Quick Punch In" enabled from the Record Menu ❸. I discussed that in a previous topic.

- ▶ **Select a Track** ❹: Just by selecting a Track, you put it, technically, into Record Enable mode, indicated by the slightly lit Record Enable Button [R] ❺. The Track has Input Focus, so when you hit the Record Button, it records on that Track. But the Track Window always has at least one Track selected so you cannot unselect that Track.
  One solution to get Logic's attention away from an Audio or Software Instrument Track is to select a Track that is not assigned to any Channel Strip (a "dead" Track ❻, no processing required). ***Ctr+click*** on a Track Header and select "No Output" ❼ from the "Reassign Track" submenu.

100 5 - Be Aware!

Conclusion

This concludes my manual *"Logic Pro X - Tips, Tricks, Secrets #1"*. If you liked it, check out Vol.2, "**Logic Pro X - Tips, Tricks, Secrets #2**" with even more topics.

If you find my visual approach of explaining features and concepts helpful, please recommend my books to others or maybe write a review on Amazon or the iBooks Store. This will help me to continue this series.

To check out other books in my "Graphically Enhanced Manuals" series, go to my website at:

www.DingDingMusic.com/Manuals

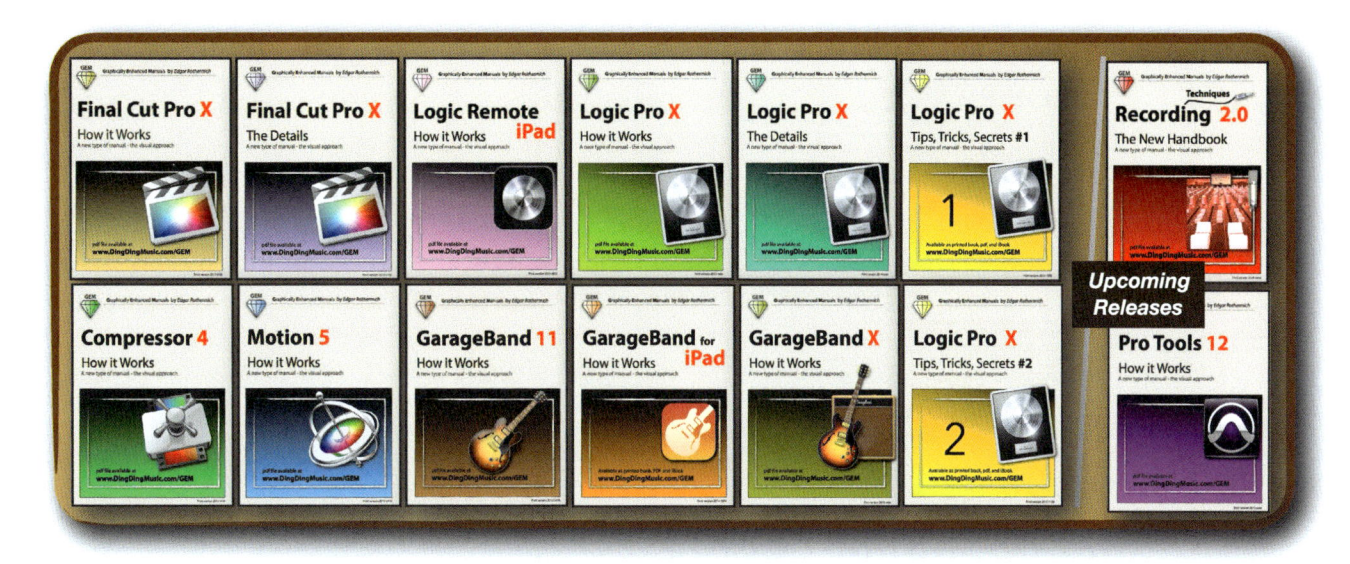

To contact me directly, email me at: GEM@DingDingMusic.com

More information about my day job as a composer and links to my social network sites are on my website:
www.DingDingMusic.com

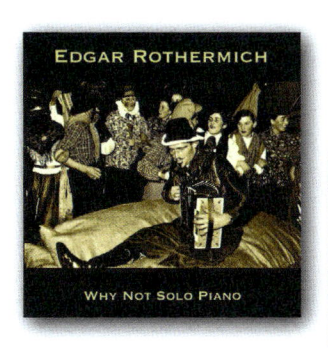

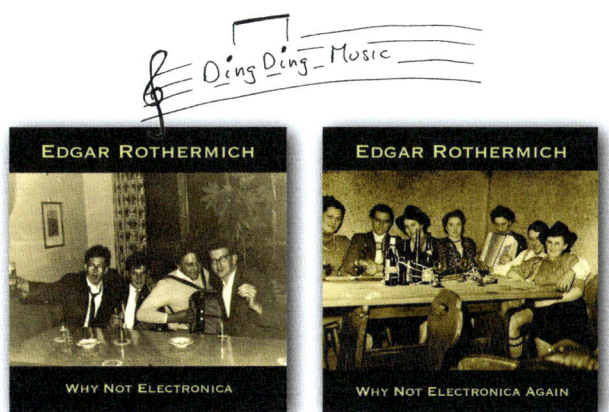

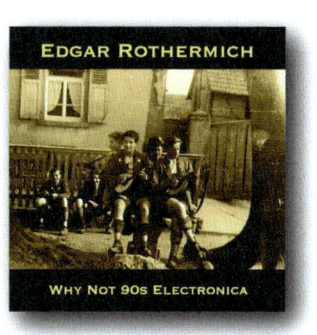

Listen to my music on SoundCloud

Thanks for your interest and your support,

Edgar Rothermich

Printed in Great Britain
by Amazon